HOW TO

FIND AND BUY A BUILDING PLOT

~

Roy Speer & Michael Dade

Publ...

AC
We
Mur
of Be .... of
East (.... .or supplying
house | ....g plans and illustrations;
the pec ....u case studies; and the chartered
surveyor. ...ure agents throughout the UK who provided
information. Special thanks to our families, Pennie, Emma,
George and Harry Speer, and Tina, Rowan and Josie Dade,
without whose support the book would not have been written.

NOTE
The authors, the publishers, their assigns, licensees and
printers cannot accept liability for any errors or omissions
contained herein nor liability for any loss to any person acting
or refraining from action as a result of the information
contained in this book. The book should not be used as a
sole reference and readers contemplating the purchase of a
building plot are advised to seek professional advice.

Names and other details given in the examples in this book
are for the purposes of illustration only. No reference to real
people and places is intended or should be inferred.

Second edition 1998 published by
Stonepound Books
10 Stonepound Road
Hassocks
West Sussex BN6 8PP 01273 842155

First published 1995 by J M Dent Ltd, London
Copyright © Roy Speer and Michael Dade 1998

A CIP catalogue record for this book is available from the
British Library.

ISBN 0 9533489 1 1

Designed by
David Edmonds Presentation, Graphics and Design
0181 295 1901

Printed and bound by XPS Limited, Brighton
01273 421242

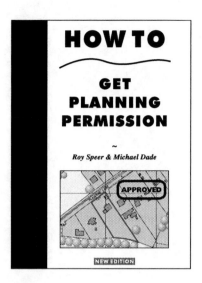

HOW TO

GET PLANNING PERMISSION

~

Roy Speer & Michael Dade

APPROVED

NEW EDITION

How to Get Planning Permission is the essential companion volume to **How to Find and Buy a Building Plot** that gives you all the information you will need on planning permission and using the planning system effectively. With over 80 illustrations, tables and examples, this book tells you

◆ how to dramatically increase your chances of success - before your application is even submitted
◆ when to make full or outline applications
◆ how to complete application forms and notices to your best advantage
◆ 9 essential points for writing a supporting letter and 8 common mistakes to avoid
◆ what you must include in application plans and drawings
◆ 8 steps to help your proposal through the application process successfully
◆ all the ways you can overcome objections and refusals
◆ 14 vital factors to take into account in applications for new homes
◆ the critical issues in applications for conversions, extensions, home improvements, demolition and re-builds, mobile homes, sub-dividing houses, buildings in your garden, working from home and agricultural dwellings
◆ how to tell whether an appeal will succeed and the crucial steps to see an appeal through
◆ how four families got their planning permissions against the odds

Order your copy of How To Get Planning Permission from your book seller or direct from Stonepound Books (01273 842155). Price £12.50, mail order £13.50.

Contents

PART 2 FINDING THE PLOT   41

CHAPTER 6 WHERE TO LOOK   43

CHAPTER 7 HIDDEN OPPORTUNITIES   52

PART 3 ASSESSING YOUR PLOT   63

CHAPTER 8 FIRST CONSIDERATIONS   65

INTRODUCTION

Many people dream of building their own home. For some it is a way of acquiring an ideal home, for others it is an economical means of providing accommodation, or even a way of making money. Every year thousands of people do build their own homes, or have one built specifically for them. The way they go about this - the amount of work they do, how the house is designed, the type of construction, where their finance comes from - varies slightly in almost every case. One of the few things all of them have in common is finding a suitable piece of land on which to build their house - probably the biggest single challenge they face. Yet good practical and informed advice is scarce and, until the first edition of **How to Find and Buy a Building Plot** was published 1995, there was no comprehensive source of information on how to find and buy land on which to build a house. This book was originally written to fill that gap.

If you plan to find and buy an existing building to convert into a new home, rather than to build a new house from scratch, most of the advice in this book is equally relevant. For simplicity's sake, we shall refer in the text just to 'building plots', but you should read this phrase to encompass conversion properties as well.

Some people build a home for themselves in the garden of their existing house. They are fortunate, as they only have to worry about planning permission, service connections, ground conditions and legal and planning restrictions, unlike the rest who face the additional hurdles of finding a plot, a rare commodity in many areas, and completing a purchase, often in the face of stiff competition. This book covers all these points and most of the content is as relevant to people who have a plot in their garden, as it is to those who do not.

For convenience, we shall frequently refer to a building plot-buyer as a 'selfbuilder' in the text, but this has a very wide meaning here. The book is intended for anyone who wants to buy a plot or build a house or convert an existing building. The information and advice apply whether you intend to build a house yourself, or have one built for you, or whether you are a builder or a professional, advising others.

How to Find and Buy a Building Plot is arranged in five Parts, each dealing with a main stage in the process. Defining requirements should be the starting point. This is often overlooked by people eager to press ahead but who usually come to grief later. Finding a plot involves looking in the usual places where plots are sold and sometimes, through necessity, in less obvious places. Having found a plot, you need to assess it to make sure that it meets your requirements with no hidden pitfalls to prevent you building. The book then turns to the key question of how much a plot is worth before looking at how to buy a plot successfully. It ends with some selfbuilders' case histories showing how three families found and bought their sites.

Your first step towards finding and buying a building plot should be to work out your requirements - size and design of house, amount of land, location and how much you can afford to spend. You need specific answers to these questions before you start looking for a plot. Buyers who define their requirements precisely and have their finance already arranged are well placed to secure a plot. Estate agents and banks or building societies do not take seriously people who seem vague about what they plan to do.

House building is about creating a new home so we shall start by considering the building itself. Usually the biggest constraint here is the budget which we deal with in Chapter 4. In practice, you will probably have to adjust both your budget and your dream home several times in order to match the two.

Whether you already have ideas about your ideal home or have a completely open mind, you need to pin your ideas down and define your requirements precisely.

DESIGN IDEAS

The best way to settle on a design is to find ideas from plans and photographs of finished houses. There is a wealth of information available. The various magazines about selfbuild and home improvement, such as *Build It* and *Individual Homes: Homebuilding and Renovating*, carry advertisements for selfbuild package companies and many of these have catalogues packed with plans and photographs. In addition, the magazines publicise shows and exhibitions. Exhibitions provide an opportunity to gather ideas and to gain an impression of the companies behind the brochures and advertisements. Major shows often feature a show house built for the occasion and walking around it is a good way of focusing your mind on what you do and do not like.

If you cannot visit a selfbuild show, there might be a show house in a new housing development nearby. Failing that, estate agents have recently-built houses on their books that you can view. During your visit, take notes, measurements and photographs.

Several useful books are available containing hundreds of house plans. Use these for inspiration and to help direct your thinking.

By these means, your eventual design will be born out of your personal preferences, which might not be catered for in a standard design.

PROFESSIONAL ADVICE

Designing houses is complex and you might need to consult a professional at some point. Drawing up detailed plans before you find a plot could mean time and money wasted, as your design should be based on the constraints and opportunities of an actual site. An informal chat with a professional before you start can help define your requirements.

You can get advice from selfbuild package companies or from independent consultants, such as building surveyors, architectural technicians or architects (to whom we will refer collectively as 'building designers'). Most of the selfbuild package companies offer flexibility in their designs and some employ professionals who can help you choose the right design. However, do not forget that they work for the company and can be restricted by the particular packages it offers. Alternatively, you can pay for independent professional advice.

The best way to find a suitable professional is by referral. Ask friends, colleagues and other professional advisers about any building designers they have used, or look in Yellow Pages directory. Check for professional qualifications: ARICS or FRICS means Chartered Surveyor; ARIBA, Chartered Architect; MSST, Surveying Technician; MBIAT, Architectural Technician; MBEng, Building Engineer. How ever you find a building designer, establish that he or she is right for the job and whether his likes or dislikes match yours. Ask to see plans and photos of previous projects. Speak to other clients. Do not only ask if they were pleased with the end result. Ask if the building designer was easy to contact, how quickly he responded and did what he was asked, and whether he had good relations with council building inspectors and planning officers.

Once you are satisfied that this is the right person for the job, brief him fully on your requirements and your budget. Agree precisely the work to be done and the fee. Get written confirmation of the figures and when payments are due.

DETAILED REQUIREMENTS

Once you have some ideas, turn them into more specific requirements. Think about the size of the house in terms of the number and dimensions of rooms. The number of bedrooms and the amount of space needed for cooking, eating and living depend on the size of your family and how often you have guests. Consider your requirements now and for the future. Do you have an expanding family or will you need a granny annexe? Think about your lifestyle. Do you entertain frequently? If so, a good-sized dining and living room are a must, complemented with an adequate hall and cloakroom. Outdoor types might need plenty of space for wellies and dogs so that a utility room next to the back door could be essential. Hobbies might need extra space, such as a darkroom, library or gym. If you work from home, you might need a study. Modern houses rarely have cellars, although they provide useful additional space for more than wine, but they can be expensive to build.

Consider the garage at an early stage. Its size will depend on its use - for storing lawn mowers, spare furniture, or as a workshop - sometimes even for parking cars. If your pride

and joy is a 1950s Cadillac, it might not fit in to a standard sized garage. Councils increasingly expect new houses with four or more bedrooms to have a double garage. The fact that you yourself have only one car, or none at all, is unlikely to sway the council if it has such a policy.

Finally, do not worry at this stage about how the layout will work. It is tempting to become distracted by design details, but this can lead you to overlook basic requirements.

HOUSE TYPES

Houses fall into three main types: house, bungalow and chalet bungalow (see Figures 1.1 to 1.7). The term 'chalet bungalow' means a two-storey building with upper rooms within, or partly within, the roof. Chalets have dormer windows or roof lights at first-floor level, and the ridge of the roof is generally lower than in traditional two-storey houses. The distinction between houses and chalets is often blurred. It is worth bearing in mind that you can sometimes build a chalet-type house on a plot originally intended for a bungalow, where you would not be able to build a full two-storey house. You can normally build a chalet on a plot intended for a house, so the choice of plot is greater if you opt for a chalet-style rather than for a house or bungalow.

LAYOUT OPTIONS

When you have worked out in broad terms what accommodation and type of house you want, you need to achieve a workable layout. Think how you would use the house. You might not want a study next to a playroom, or guests moving from living room to dining room via the kitchen, but you might need a spare bedroom on the ground floor if elderly relatives stay. Outline ideas are all you need

FIGURE 1.1 Ringdove Cottage, a four-bedroom house from the Medina Gimson Village House range

at this stage. Ultimately, you will probably work with a building designer or selfbuild package company to achieve an ideal layout or perhaps find one 'off the peg'.

Sketch your outline ideas on paper. This helps to calculate the floor area of the house accurately. The example plan and calculations show how this is done (see Figure 1.8). You now have a rough floor area for your house, but this omits the area of internal walls. For most purposes, floor area is calculated as the area enclosed by the internal surfaces of the external walls, so round up your rough calculation to reflect this.

FIGURE 1.2 The Acacia, a three bedroom bungalow from the Scandia-Hus Country Collection (© Scandia-Hus Ltd)

FIGURE 1.3 The Acacia's floor plan (© Scandia-Hus Ltd)

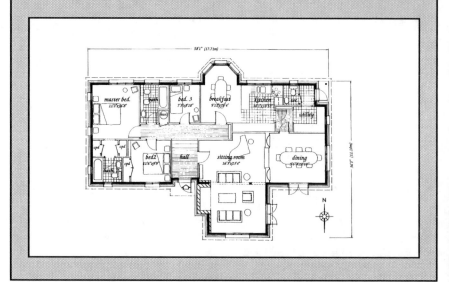

FIGURE 1.4 The Comberton, a four bedroom chalet style house from the Potton Heritage range (© Potton 1981)

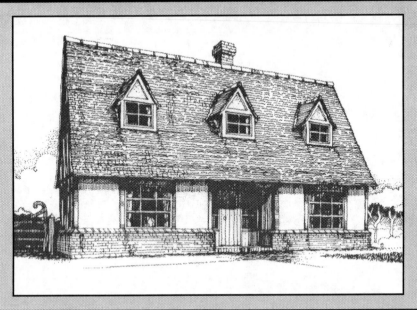

FIGURE 1.5 The Comberton's floor plans (© Potton 1981)

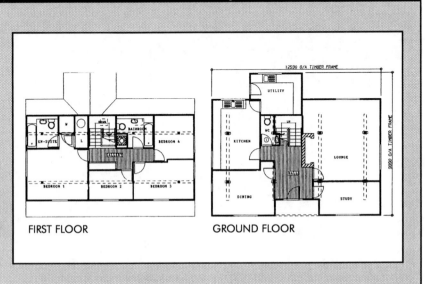

FIRST FLOOR   GROUND FLOOR

FIGURE 1.6 The Hanson Priory, a five-bedroom house from Custom Homes

FIGURE 1.7 The Hanson Priory's floor plans

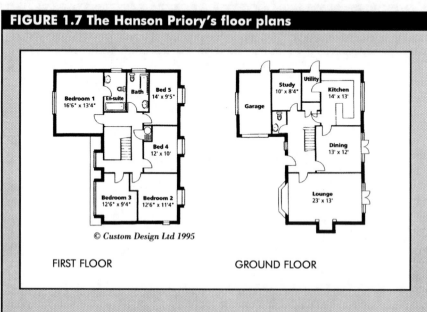

© Custom Design Ltd 1995

FIRST FLOOR   GROUND FLOOR

FIGURE 1.8 Floor plans with room dimensions and calculation of internal areas

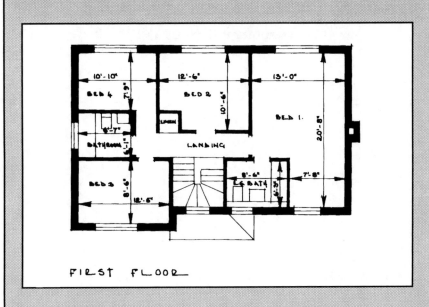

FIRST FLOOR

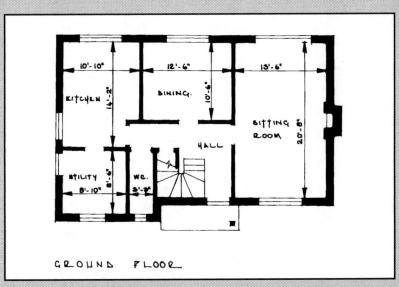

GROUND FLOOR

CALCULATION OF FLOOR AREA

	width (ft/in)		depth (ft/in)		sq ft	sq m
Ground Floor						
Kitchen	10' 10"	x	14' 2"	=	153	14
Dining room	12' 6"	x	10' 6"	=	131	12
Sitting room	13' 6"	x	20' 8"	=	279	26
Utility room	8' 10"	x	8' 6"	=	75	7
Wc	3' 3"	x	8' 6"	=	28	3
Hall/stairs					134	12
Total ground floor					**800**	**74**
First Floor						
Bedroom 1	13' 6"	x	20' 8"			
less	5' 4"	x	6' 3"	=	245	22
Bedroom 2	12' 6"	x	10' 6"	=	131	12
Bedroom 3	12' 5"	x	8' 6"	=	106	10
Bedroom 4	10' 10"	x	7' 9"	=	84	8
En suite bathroom	8' 6"	x	6' 3"	=	53	5
Bathroom	6' 7"	x	6' 1"	=	40	4
Landing/stairs					141	13
Total first floor					**800**	**74**
Total floor area					**1,600**	**148**

Floor area is an essential tool in working out the build cost, and can form the basis for discussions with a building designer or selfbuild package company. When sketching ideas, remember the stairs. Having fitted them into the ground floor plan, consider where they will emerge upstairs. In a chalet-style house stairs must avoid sloping ceilings to provide enough headroom. You also need to allow for functional space for fitted wardrobes, cupboards, airing cupboard, boiler, etc. Think about the garage: it could be integral (built into the house), possibly with first-floor rooms above; it could be attached at the side, front or even back of the house or completely detached.

The design and layout of your house is a matter of personal preference, tempered by practical constraints. Getting value for money, and planning permission, are two hurdles which can trip the more adventurous. Compared with traditional designs, unusual houses often cost more to build and appeal to a smaller market. Similarly, not every council is sympathetic to bold architectural statements, especially when they are built in glass and stainless steel.

The best way to arrive at your ideal design is to work from the inside outwards. Think about the quality of living space you want: light and airy, or warm and cosy; a cottagey feel, or something more formal. Such general points influence matters like ceiling heights and the size and numbers of windows.

For the external appearance of the house there is a wide choice of design and materials. In practice, your choice might be limited, as not every design is suitable for every site. This is something councils take into account when deciding whether to give planning permission. Planning permission is a vital element in buying a building plot which we look at in Part Three. For design purposes bear in mind that styles and materials vary across the country. A stone house with a slate roof can look out of place in a village built of bricks and clay tiles.

Final decisions on design will ultimately be influenced by the location and surroundings of your plot. By all means have an ideal, but keep one or two alternative ideas to hand. An over-rigid approach will restrict the number of plots that meet your requirements.

ORGANISING CONSTRUCTION

Your chosen way of carrying out the project will have a bearing on the cost of the house and its design and, ultimately, on finding and buying the right plot. The options fall into five broad categories:

◆ **Building-designer-led project:** The designer co-ordinates and oversees the project, from preparing the plans to supervising the build.
◆ **Complete design and build package, also known as a 'turn-key' package:** A specialist company undertakes the entire project, sometimes including site-finding and buying.
◆ **Project management package:** A project manager organises and oversees the build on your behalf.
◆ **Self-managed, labour sub-contracted:** You manage the project, hiring and co-ordinating sub-contractors to do all the building work.
◆ **Self-managed, selfbuild:** You do everything, acting as both builder and project manager.

These are not clear-cut categories and selfbuilders often use a combination to complete their project. As a general rule, the more work you do yourself, the cheaper the build will be. This might release more money for a bigger or better plot. The greater your own involvement in the construction or its supervision, the more accessible you must be to the site. Trying to co-ordinate several teams of sub-contractors by car phone is unlikely to produce the desired results in the right time. However, accessibility might narrow your area of search making it harder to find a plot.

CONSTRUCTION METHODS

Most houses are built of timber frame or brick and block, although reinforced concrete and steel frame construction are both viable alternatives. Cost, speed of build, flexibility of design and thermal efficiency are some of the factors to consider in choosing which method to use. The type of construction is unlikely to affect your choice of plot and will not be considered when you apply for planning permission.

CHAPTER 2   THE PLOT

Once you have an idea of what you want to build, think about the building plot. Your plot has to accommodate:

◆ House
◆ Garage
◆ Access drive and turning area
◆ Front garden
◆ Back garden
◆ Outbuildings

SIZE OF PLOT

The size of house and garage determines the minimum width or 'frontage' of the plot. Allow at least 1 m (3ft 3ins) between the sides of the house and each boundary for maintenance of walls, gutters and roof. You can build foundations right up to a boundary but this might create a maintenance problem, as you could not maintain the wall, gutter or roof, without going onto neighbouring land. You might also meet resistance from the council if you try to squeeze your house into too tight a space, as the Building Regulations impose minimum wall-to-boundary distances, especially where the wall has windows and doors. The minimum plot frontage you need, then, is the width of the house, plus the width of the garage, plus at least 3 m (10 ft). Also allow a gap between the house and the garage. On some plots a detached garage in front of the house is suitable. This allows a narrower plot, but can spoil views from front windows. An alternative for a narrow plot is an integral garage.

Councils' parking standards for new houses generally require at least two off-street parking spaces. For a family-sized house, ideally allow two spaces (probably in the garage) plus enough space for children's and visitors' cars.

The type of road your plot has access to may mean providing an on-site turning area so that cars do not have to back out into traffic. This is essential for plots on major or through roads. Access without a turning area is usually allowed only for a cul-de-sac or no through road. Turning areas require space which has to be allowed for in your plot. Access is important and can be a complex matter; it is fully explained in Part Three.

The size of garden you need depends on how you plan to use it. Do you entertain in the garden, play sports, or grow fruit and vegetables? A gardening enthusiast might want greenhouses and potting sheds. Other requirements can include space for patio, workshop, conservatory, swimming pool or tennis court. You might need to allow for trees, shrubs and fences to provide privacy. Do not overlook functional areas like washing lines, dustbins, and compost bins - all take up space.

If you keep horses you might want a paddock. Note that a '3.25 acre plot' and a '0.25 acre plot plus 3 acre paddock' are very different. A 3.25 acre plot suggests scope for a very large house which will be priced accordingly. A 0.25 acre plot plus paddock is just that, although the paddock will add to the price of the plot.

Once you have a clear idea of your requirements for the outside, calculate the area and frontage of the plot you need to accommodate them (see Figure 2.1). A sketch plan (see Figure 2.2) will be helpful and more so if you draw it to scale. A scale of 1:200 is fairly straightforward: each metre on the ground is represented by half a centimetre on the page. A plan may seem unnecessary at this stage, but is useful when you come to work out whether your house will actually fit a particular plot.

FIGURE 2.1 Plot dimensions and areas

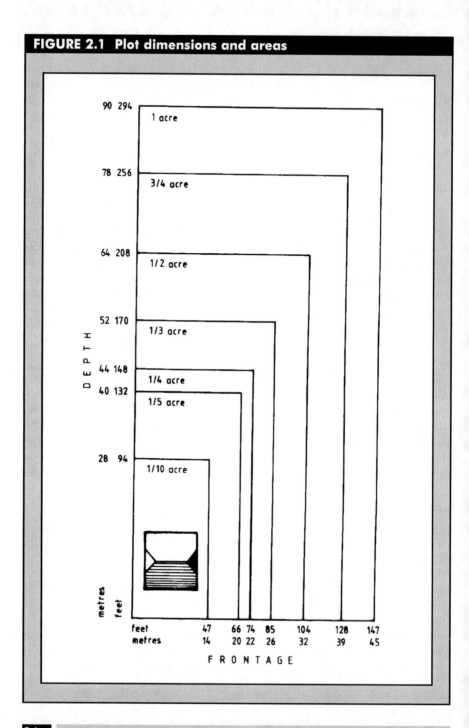

FIGURE 2.2 Half acre (0.91 hectare) plot, showing the space needed for the various elements that might be fitted in

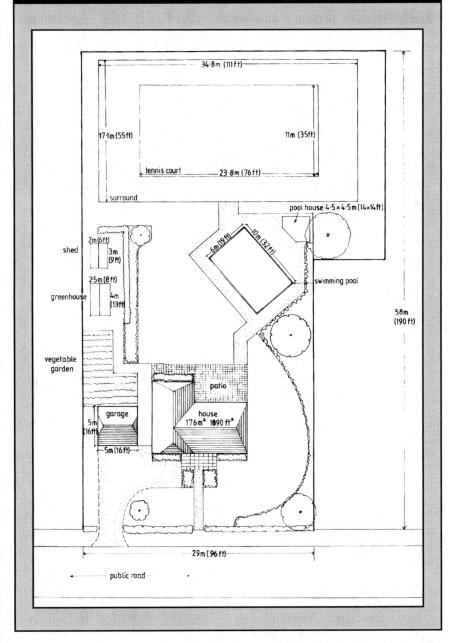

34·8m (111 ft)

17·1m (55 ft)

11m (35ft)

tennis court — 23·8m (76 ft)

surround

pool house 4·5 × 4·5 m (14×14 ft)

2m (6ft)

shed

3m (9ft)

6m (19 ft) 10m (32 ft)

2·5m (8 ft)

greenhouse

4m (13ft)

swimming pool

58m (190 ft)

vegetable garden

patio

5m (16ft)

garage

house 176 m² 1890 ft²

5m (16 ft)

29m (96 ft)

public road

FIGURES 2.3 and 2.4 Urban plot and garden plot

Building plots come in all shapes, sizes and places, from large gardens in villages for a cottage to urban redevelopment sites for a town house. Decide what type and character of plot you want before you start your search.

PLOT CHARACTERISTICS

Plots come in all shapes and sizes and not all the parts can necessarily be used. An irregular shape, steeply sloping ground or the presence of trees or other obstacles, might mean that you need a larger total area than your initial calculations suggest.

The character of plots varies from small urban infill sites to acres of isolated countryside (see Figures 2.3 and 2.4). Plots can be individual, part of a small group, or part of an estate of new houses. A coastal plot could be little more than a patch of shingle, a rural plot could be overgrown woodland, and an urban plot could be occupied by dilapidated buildings. Many plots are created from existing large gardens. Established trees and hedges add instant character and reduce landscaping costs. They can, however, add to building costs and restrict the choice of site layouts. The opposite extreme, bare land, might need extensive landscaping but it is straightforward to lay out and build.

The land may be level or steeply sloping. Often, because of ill-defined or overgrown boundaries, it is hard to see a plot there at all. Sometimes sites look deceptively small, just as the footprint of a house does when pegged out on the ground. Whatever the existing character of the plot, you will change it radically with your house, drive, access and garden. Ultimately it is you who shapes the character of your plot.

Definite ideas on the size, location and character of plot you want are an invaluable aid to finding the right site. As with house design, it does not pay to be too rigid in your thinking. Many people start with unrealistic expectations of what their money will buy. Look at plots for sale and plots where new houses have been built. New detached houses on estates marketed with 'generous' or 'spacious' gardens rarely occupy more than a fifth of an acre, yet this accommodates an 1,800 sq ft house, double garage and garden. Be wary of agents' descriptions of plot sizes: 'about 0.5 acre', can turn out to be nearer one third of an acre, despite the Property Misdescriptions Act of 1991.

CHAPTER 3   THE LOCATION

There is an old saying in the property business that the three most important factors in assessing land are: location, location and location. This is true of building plots.

You can change a plot by landscaping and by adding or removing buildings. Homes can be extended, decorated, given a new cladding, or even pulled down and rebuilt in a different style. The location of a plot is permanent.

Building your own home involves: finding finance; buying a plot; choosing a house; obtaining planning permission; and building and fitting out. The process involves an enormous commitment of time, energy and money. It is vitally important that you invest this in the right location. Do not wait until the house is complete before finding out that there is an hour's drive to the nearest school, that buses do not run from the place where family and friends live, or that it is down wind from a pig farm.

THE COUNTRYSIDE

Plots are found wherever there are opportunities to get planning permission to build - from town centres to deepest countryside. Modern planning regulations date from 1948. Before that, development occurred in a much more piecemeal fashion. Local and national planning policies now dictate that new housing in the countryside is strictly limited. 'Countryside', for planning purposes, is land outside the limits of cities, towns and villages as defined in councils' Local Plans. This means that rural hamlets, small villages and suburban fringes can be classified as 'countryside', even if they comprise large amounts of housing and other buildings.

FIGURE 3.1 Suburban infill plot

There are far more opportunities to build in existing towns and villages, such as this suburban infill plot, where councils' planning policies generally allow new housing. Within these areas, character varies widely between densely built-up central locations, modern housing estates and more spacious suburbs.

FIGURE 3.2 Rural plot

In most rural areas, although the demand for new building is high, the scope is strictly limited by planning policies. Plots do come up, particularly when there are gaps in groups of houses, as in this case where the planning application site notice can be seen on the fence post.

Opportunities do exist in the countryside, perhaps to replace a derelict house or where an old planning permission has been kept alive over the years. In very limited circumstances, operators of agricultural businesses can gain planning permission to build houses. This is dealt with in Chapter 12. Some rural plots can be subject to an 'agricultural tie', restricting occupation of the house to someone working in or retired from agriculture.

TOWNS AND VILLAGES

In towns and larger villages, council planning policies generally allow new housing. Available plots are common in areas of sparse or irregular housing on the edge of towns. Victorian houses with very large gardens provide opportunities for infilling. Small houses on big plots offer scope for replacement houses or sub-division. Paddocks and orchards also provide opportunities for plots.

Areas of large-scale new development can also yield single plots. Developers and councils sometimes sell individual plots to selfbuilders. These can be redevelopment sites in town centres or greenfield sites on the edge of towns.

Commercial sites, especially in or near residential areas, can get planning permission for building plots. These include former garages and pubs, builder's yards, small factories and nursery gardens.

AREA OF SEARCH

Finding the location right for you involves first defining the area where you want to live. You can then concentrate your search within that area for plots that meet your practical and

FIGURE 3.3 Area of search plan

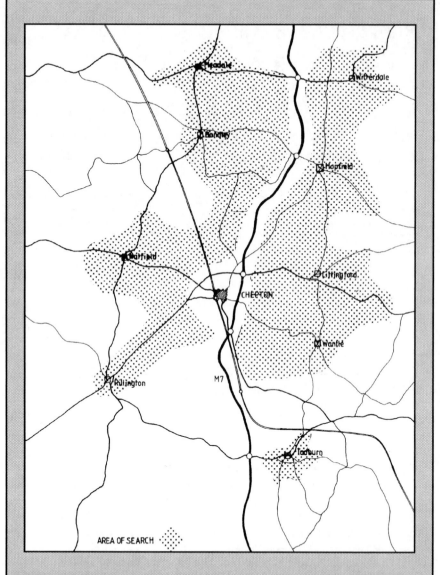

Get a map of the area and mark on it all the places where you would want to live. Use the map as the basis of your search and to brief estate agents and others on your requirements.

aesthetic requirements, from which you can make a final choice.

Defining your area of search demands a careful examination of all aspects of your life. Factors that influence the choice of location can include: where your friends and family live; where you have lived previously; where you work; your type of work; whether you have children at school; where shopping, social and leisure facilities are; and access to road, rail and airport links. Consider each in terms of travelling time. From this a pattern should emerge and you can begin to define an area. Plot these key locations on a map (see Figure 3.3). Do not simply draw a circle around one point, say, a ten-mile radius of your optimum location. Your defined area will probably be irregularly shaped. Exclude all locations where you definitely do not want to live. Draw your area of search as widely as possible to give yourself maximum scope. In areas of short supply, some plot-buyers settle for a different county from the one in which they started looking.

If you want to live in the countryside and nowhere else, your choice is going to be restricted compared with a buyer who will accept town or village locations. If you have very particular requirements, like a river frontage or a spectacular view, your choice will be restricted still further. To increase your choice of plots, widen your area of search. Your quest for the right plot could, however, distance you from family, friends, or schools. Consequently, a thorough analysis of your priorities is essential to define a realistic area of search.

INFLUENCES ON CHOICE

Keep in mind the geography of the area and the surrounding uses. High ground can be windy or liable to snow or fog. Low-lying ground can flood or, again, be windy if it is open and exposed. A plot near the coast might be appealing in summer but bleak and miserable in winter. Motorways and airports are noisy, and even rural roads can become choked with holiday traffic in summer. A lively seaside town may be dead out-of-season. Industry, power stations, and rubbish tips could have noise, health and traffic implications. Even an idyllic rural area might suffer from farmyard noise and smell, or be so quiet as to create a sense of isolation in those used to urban bustle.

Advice on plot hunting sometimes emphasises the need to compromise and be realistic in your expectations. Be realistic by all means, but do not take this too far. If there are few plots available in your area of search, you may either have to accept a long wait for the right plot, or compromise on your requirements. If your enjoyment of your dream home will be constantly marred by the roar of traffic from a main road, wait for a quieter plot elsewhere. Your willingness to compromise might depend on how long you plan to live in the house.

Finally, think about the social implications of your chosen location as not every community welcomes outsiders with open arms. This only applies in a small number of cases, but if you do not know the area already, find out about it before buying a plot there.

Having looked at the factors that influence where you want to live, keep in mind the cost and availability of plots as plot prices vary enormously across Britain. The budget for a two-bedroom bungalow on a small but select plot in Surrey might stretch to a four-bedroom house with several acres of unspoilt countryside in the Western Isles of Scotland.

How do you know what you can afford to spend on a building plot? To answer this vital question you need to work out a budget covering the purchase of the plot and the construction of the house itself. When you start looking for plots and when the time comes to make an offer, you must be certain about how much you can afford and that the money will be available when it is needed. Of course, until you find a plot you cannot be certain about basic details like final design or foundation costs. Prepare a draft budget like the one in Figure 4.1 at this stage and you can firm it up as your plans progress. This is time well spent as overspending on the perfect plot might put building your dream home financially out of reach.

THE DRAFT BUDGET

There are three basic elements in a draft budget:

◆ The cost of the build
◆ The cost of the plot
◆ Available finance

Clearly, the first two figures must total less than the third for your project to be viable. If you know roughly the size of house you want to build, you can work out an approximate build cost. You can find out the level of plot prices in the area of your search. Add these figures to estimate the amount of money you have to find. Alternatively, look at the equation the other way round. From the finance available, deduct the build cost to arrive at the sum you can spend on a plot. Your draft budget can start life on the back of an envelope as a guesstimate of what you can

afford. To pin down more precisely how much money you can spend on a plot, or what size house you can afford to build, look more closely at each of the main elements.

FINANCE OPTIONS

First, look at your total available finance. This is normally made up of:

◆ The equity in your existing house (value of the house less any outstanding mortgage).
◆ Any capital you or your family have available.
◆ The amount you can raise by a new mortgage or loan.

In assessing remaining equity in your existing house do not forget to deduct costs of sale - agents' commission, solicitors' fees and removal expenses. Take account of market conditions, be realistic about how much your house will fetch and remember that asking prices are not necessarily selling prices. Check your estimate with local estate agents who are usually happy to give a valuation in the hope of gaining your instructions when the time comes to sell.

If you are adding any capital into the budget, get advice on the most tax-efficient way to use it and what proportion to put in.

Where you need to take out a new mortgage or loan, look at all the options, as there are now many different schemes and your individual circumstances will determine which is the most suitable. The main sources of finance for building your own home are banks and building societies. Most are fully aware of selfbuild and able to offer help and

FIGURE 4.1 Draft budgets

1 Calculating the total funds required to buy a plot and build your house

Plot price, including fees	35,000
Estimated building costs, including contingency	65,000
Total funds required	£100,000

2 Calculating what size house you can afford to build

Maximum amount of funds available	100,000
Plot price, including fees	(35,000)
Amount available for building house	65,000
Allow for building cost @ £40 per sq ft	
Maximum size of house in sq ft (65,000÷40) =	1,600 sq ft

3 Calculating how much you can afford to spend on a plot

Maximum amount of funds available	100,000
Estimated building costs, including contingency	(65,000)
Maximum amount available for plot and fees	£35,000

advice either through their branches or a specialist selfbuild finance department. Some offer finance packages aimed at people building their own homes, others devise a specific scheme tailor-made for your needs.

Most lenders expect you to put your equity in at the start of the project to fund or part fund the plot purchase. The lender then makes staged payments to cover the construction work. In the rising property market of the late 1980s selfbuild mortgages often allowed people to stay in their existing house while the new house was being built. This is now very rare, although one or two lenders still consider such an arrangement where a current mortgage is low and the equity input is high. In most cases, therefore, when you locate a suitable plot, your lender is likely to expect you to sell your existing house before making the finance available.

All lenders have their own lending criteria, so check the small print carefully. Points to look for include:

◆ Restrictions on the 'age' of the planning permission on the plot - a permission that expires within a year or two might not be acceptable.
◆ Restrictions on the start and finish dates of your build.
◆ Stage payments during the build - check whether the lender's stages tie in with the

FIGURE 4.2 Typical costs of building a home

Example 1

◆ Bungalow, 3 bedrooms, 1,600 sq ft, brick and block, double garage, owner doing all building work

Soil test	750
Foundations and drains	4,250
Building materials	5,385
Roofing	2,750
Internal finishes and fittings	5,850
Service connections	1,500
Kitchen, bathroom and decorations	2,500
Miscellaneous	5,000
Professional fees	3,750
Building costs	31,735
Plot	23,235
Total cost	**£54,970**

Example 2

◆ Chalet, 3 bedrooms, 1,800 sq ft, timber frame, double garage, owner doing some building work

Timber frame and erection	44,000
Foundations	6,000
Bricks, blocks and bricklayer	3,650
Garage	5,000
Roof tiles and labour	4,200
Plumbing, electrics, heating system	6,400
Scaffolding and equipment hire	1,200
Connection charges	900
Sundries	1,150
Professional fees	1,250
Building costs	73,750
Plot	53,500
Total cost	**£127,250**

The Budget

FIGURE 4.2 Typical costs of building a home Cont...

Example 3

◆ Two storey, 4 bedrooms, 2,300 sq ft, traditional build, double garage, owner
doing no building work

Building materials	53,500
Drainage	1,080
Bricklayer, carpenter and roofer	12,700
Electrics, plumbing, decorator, plasterer	14,670
Landscaping and paving	4,100
Scaffolding and plant hire	1,750
Connection charges	1,960
Professional fees and insurance	2,230
Building costs	91,990
Plot	61,250
Total cost	**£153,240**

stages at which your builder or package company needs to be paid.

◆ Restrictions on who builds, the type of structural warranty and provisions for insurance.

Whatever your situation, a chat with your bank, building society or financial adviser is a good starting point to sort out your method of finance but do shop around for the best deal for your particular circumstances.

BUILD COST

The next step is to look more closely at the build cost (see Figure 4.2). Get a rough figure, based on a price per sq ft, from a builder, building designer or selfbuild package company. A very useful book on construction and building costs is The House Builder's Bible by Mark Brinkley (01223 290230). Selfbuild magazines and selfbuild package companies'

brochures give current price levels. These are a good starting point, but you must check how the figures are made up - whether they include: professional fees; cost of service connections; foundations; garage; drive, fencing and landscaping; or insurance. Budgets for kitchens and bathrooms can be modest. Brochures include rough costings based on ideal scenarios - a level, serviced plot; good soil conditions; existing access; and fenced boundaries - but you might not be so lucky. Add any missing elements plus a contingency figure of at least 5 per cent to cover any unforeseen expenses.

You will pay VAT on building materials although in some cases you can claim this back when the project is complete. Make sure that VAT is accounted for in your budget because, even if you can get the VAT back, there is still a significant impact on your cash flow in the meantime.

PLOT PRICE

For an idea of the likely cost of a building plot, contact estate agents in the area of your search. Tell them what type of house you want to build and the sort of location you are looking for. If you already have a builder, building designer or selfbuild package company, they might be able to give you an indication of current price levels for plots.

ADJUSTING THE FIGURES

Once you have preliminary figures for plot and building costs, compare these with the amount of money you have available for the project. If the figures look tight at this stage, think about the implications. Your estimated build costs are more likely to increase than decrease as the project progresses. Examine your priorities carefully. If a particular house type is your overriding priority, cost this accurately and then see what is left for the plot. Consider whether that figure will buy a plot of adequate size in the right location. If it will not, decide whether you are prepared to look further afield or to spend the additional time and effort to find the right plot at a bargain price. Alternatively, a change of house type might produce savings that could be allocated to the plot, making a quick purchase more likely.

Spend time drafting a realistic budget. It will help you to focus on how you will finance the project, the size and type of house, how the house will be built and all the associated costs. But, most important for you at this stage, it shows you how much you can afford to spend on your plot.

Having decided what you want to build and where, how you want to set about the project, how much it is all going to cost and how you are going to fund it, you are now ready to find and buy a building plot. Buying a plot is not like buying a house or even a car. A plot's value lies in the sort of house it can accommodate, rather than in the land itself. Understanding what determines plot prices will help you in your search.

PLANNING PERMISSIONS

A building plot is development land, the value of which is determined by its planning permission. Many plots are sold with the benefit of outline planning permission which establishes the principle that some sort of dwelling can be built on the plot. Detailed or full planning permission is for a specific size and design of house, the full details of which are all part of the permission. Both types of planning permission create development value in the plot. If a plot has planning permission for, say, a bungalow or a modest three-bedroom house, its value is less than if the permission is for a large five-bedroom house.

In practice things are not always so simple. Existing planning permissions do not always reflect the full potential of the plot. A plot with permission for a two-bedroom house and worth £20,000 might actually be viable for a four-bedroom luxury house with a plot value of £40,000. The person who achieves the additional value is the one who spots and exploits the potential. This could be the existing owner or it could be an astute purchaser who buys and then gets a new planning permission. Occasionally, a plot has planning permission for one house but is large enough for two or three - the sort of opportunity which property developers dream

of. Although your prime motivation might be to build your dream home, do not ignore the possibility of stumbling on a gold mine.

A common misconception is that one can simply buy a piece of agricultural land for £1,000 or £2,000, obtain planning permission and create a building plot. If land has no planning permission, but there is potential for obtaining it, this is normally reflected in the price. Where a plot lies outside a residential area, its price can be affected by its potential for other uses, for example offices next door might desperately need more floor space or extra parking. The price the owners would pay for adjoining land suitable for their purposes could be higher than its value as a building plot.

EFFECTS ON VALUE

The value of a plot depends on what can be built on it, less the cost of carrying out that building. A range of practical considerations can affect the cost of developing a plot and, therefore, its value - ground conditions, services, access problems - and Part Three covers all these in detail. Anything that adds unusual cost to the build, or restricts how a plot can be developed, should be reflected in the price. At the time that a plot is put on the market the vendors might be unaware of problems that could come to light and affect the eventual sale price. It is for buyers to investigate plots thoroughly.

Market conditions have a profound effect on the value of plots and, as with any commodity, supply and demand are the determining forces. The plot market is very closely linked to the fortunes of the housing market, with national fluctuations, and regional, county and local variations. These affect price levels and also supply and demand for different sectors of the market, like detached houses or terraced houses.

In a buoyant housing market building plots become attractive to developers, builders and speculators. Plot prices rise, fuelled by demand and the prospect of house prices rising during the time taken to build the house. In these conditions, selfbuilders are at a disadvantage unless they enter the market fully prepared.

You may not be aiming to sell your finished house for profit, but you can still lose out to builders and developers even though they have to allow for a profit in their calculations. Builders can promise the estate agent who sells them a plot, the handling of the sale of the finished house in return. The opportunity to earn another commission gives estate agents a powerful incentive to sell to builders. Some agents automatically offer any plots they have only to a few favoured builders. Established builders can show a good track record of paying a fair price, buying quickly and being reliable. In comparison you are an unknown quantity who will only be taken seriously if you are thoroughly prepared and give the impression that you know exactly what you are doing.

A depressed housing market is often a much more fertile environment for selfbuilders. Builders and developers are cautious, their bids for plots reflect the low price they might get for the finished house and the risk that they might not be able to sell at all. You have no such worries, provided that you can sell your existing house, and can often outbid any builders. You have less time pressure: you can assess the plot thoroughly, obtain your planning permission and double-check your budget before committing yourself

to the purchase.

Good sites are always in demand, whatever the state of the market. Plots of half an acre or more in a rural or semi-rural setting, not too far from shops or station, and perhaps with a view, fetch surprisingly high prices in even the most depressed market. Similarly, plots in select small towns and villages, noted perhaps for their old world charm, attract much higher prices than those in other less favoured towns or villages nearby.

Whatever the state of the market, never pay a price higher than your personal estimation of the value of the plot. Asking prices can be very misleading: in a busy market they are frequently exceeded, sometimes by large margins, and in a quiet market they can be hopelessly optimistic. Often no firm asking price is quoted, instead offers are invited or a guide price is given. This emphasises that it is for you to make an offer which the seller will then accept or reject.

PRICE GUIDE

We look at how to value a plot in Part Four, but to estimate the price you will have to pay, watch the market. Get a general idea of price levels from several estate agents who sell plots in your area of search. Try to talk to other people who have bought plots recently. You will soon discover the level of local prices. Look at your budget again to work out a general price guide for yourself which should not be within narrow bands. If you have £50,000 available for the plot, set your price guide nearer £70,000 to ensure that when you set out to find a plot you do not miss overpriced plots which may have been on the market for many months.

DEFINING YOUR REQUIREMENTS - CHECK LIST

Before you start looking for your plot, write down answers to these questions. Use the completed check list as the basis for your search and for briefing estate agents and others on your requirements.

◆ **Preferred size and type of house**
   Type (bungalow/chalet/house) . . . . *CHALET*
   Number of bedrooms *4*
   Total floor area (sq ft) *1600*
   Style of house . . . . *TRADITIONAL*

◆ **Size of plot**
   Minimum frontage . . . . *100 FT*
   Area (acres) *0.5*

◆ **Type and location of plot**
   Setting (town/village/country) . . . . *VILLAGE*
   Type (individual/group/estate) . . . . *INDIVIDUAL*

◆ **Area of search**
   List all towns and villages within area of search . . . .
   . . . .

◆ **Source of finance**
   Equity in existing house . . . .
   Capital available . . . .
   Maximum mortgage/loan . . . .
   Name of bank/building society . . . .

◆ **Preliminary budget**
   Available finance *200*
   Estimated total building costs *150*
   Amount available for plot *50*

◆ **Price guide for plot**
   Approx. minimum . . . . *30 -40*
   Approx. maximum . . . . *60 -70*

Building plots for sale can be few and far between. Plots vary enormously in area, character and price and in their suitability for the size and type of house you intend to build. If you want some degree of choice - or in some areas to find a plot at all - you need to investigate as many different sources as possible.

Good plots sell quickly as builders and developers seek out the really prime sites. Only problem plots stay on the market for months or years. You will probably not find a perfect plot on the market the moment you start looking. You might be lucky, but more likely you will have to use some of the plot-finding methods suggested here.

CHAPTER 6 WHERE TO LOOK

In this chapter we look at where most plots are sold or advertised, which is where you should start your search.

ESTATE AGENTS

Most plots are sold through estate agents except in Scotland where sales are shared equally between estate agents and solicitors. Scottish solicitors operate property centres, like large estate agents' offices, where houses and plots are sold. Unlike estate agents, property centres advertise all sites being sold by solicitors in the area. In the South of England and Home Counties plots are not usually widely advertised by agents in the same way as houses are, although in the West, Midlands and North this is quite normal. Not all estate agents deal with the sale of plots; of those that do, some have specialist land departments, while others sell only one or two plots a year.

If you are plot hunting in an area you do not know, look in Yellow Pages for the names and telephone numbers of local estate agents. Start with the large multi-office practices and with firms of chartered surveyors who are involved in estate agency as these usually offer a wide range of property services. Not all large estate agents deal in plots, but those that do may well have a wide selection. If these firms do not deal with plots, they should be able to point you in the right direction.

Most estate agents who regularly sell plots keep an applicants register with details of people who are looking and the type and location of plots they want. Agents generally have a form to be filled in and this information is held on a database. To be included on the register, you can telephone, call in or write to agents, but your best bet is to do all three. Telephone to make an appointment, go to the meeting with a clear definition of your requirements, and follow up afterwards with a letter confirming your ability to make a quick and sensible offer for the right piece of land. This marks you out as a serious buyer and distinguishes you from many people who turn up with only the vaguest idea of what they are looking for and how much they can afford to spend. Register with all agents who sell plots in your area of search.

Once registered with agents, remind them of your interest regularly. If the agent has a steady turnover of plots and advertises regularly, ring a day or two before the advertisements are published to get ahead of any competition.

Remember, estate agents owe buyers nothing as they work for, and are paid by, the vendor - the person for whom they sell the plot. The amount of help and information you get from agents can vary widely. Some are willing and able to give you information about planning permission and services (drainage, gas, water, electricity). Others give no more than brief particulars showing the location of the site often with phrases like 'it is for the purchaser to satisfy himself as to the position and availability of services', and 'all enquiries regarding planning should be addressed to the Local Planning Authority'.

Some agents send out particulars of sites which they are not directly instructed to sell which means, if you successfully buy such a plot, that the agent expects you to pay his fee, not the vendor. This should be clearly stated on the particulars along with the agents' fee or commission. If you are interested in the plot, contact the agent first to establish exactly what fee you would be liable for and when, if you went ahead and bought the plot. In these

FIGURE 6.1 Agents' particulars

BALLINGTONS
The Estate Agents

FOR SALE
BUILDING PLOT

Oak Tree Lane, Hancton

Description: The plot has an open southerly aspect with views of the sea. It extends to one third of an acre with a frontage of 60 feet and a depth of about 250 feet. A former paddock, the plot is mostly laid to grass with established trees and shrubs along the northern boundary.

Planning: Outline planning permission was granted at appeal dated 13th September 1998, under application number HN/109/98, for the erection of one dwelling.

Services: All main services are understood to be available. The purchaser is advised to contact the utility companies regarding connections.

Terms: The purchaser will be responsible for erecting a 6ft close board fence along the southern boundary of the site within one month of completion of the sale or before commencement of the building works, whichever is sooner.

Location: From this office turn left along High Street and take the third right into Oak Tree Lane. The plot will be found 1.5 miles down the lane on the left.

Viewing: Strictly by appointment with Ballingtons.

Price: Offers are invited for the Freehold, in the region of £45,000.

Ballingtons, for themselves and for the Vendors, give notice that these particulars are produced in good faith and are a general guide only and do not form part of a Contract. No person employed by Ballingtons has authority to make or give any representation or warranty in relation to this property.

Offices also at: Aberfall, Llanfern, Lunford Cross, Maerdon, Sapley Common and Monton

Agents' particulars vary widely in content and accuracy. This example shows the amount of information typically available. Plot particulars may include a photograph or ordnance survey extract.

FIGURE 6.2 Abbreviations used in estate agents' advertisements and sales particulars

PP	Planning Permission
OPP	Outline Planning Permission
DPP	Detailed Planning Permission
FPP	Full Planning Permission
F/H	Freehold
L/H	Leasehold
OIRO	Offers In the Region Of
ONO	Or Nearest Offer

circumstances the agent is working for you, and might do more work on your behalf, to earn his fee, including obtaining planning documents, checking availability and cost of service connections and negotiating the price.

Agents' particulars are the butt of many jokes - 'good transport links to major cities' means next to a motorway; 'convenient for the airport' means at the end of the runway; 'land with potential' means a plot without planning permission. The Property Misdescriptions Act (1991) was passed to put an end to such entertaining use of language. No matter how accurate particulars appear to be, you should always check for yourself any claims made and information given and watch out for omissions (see Figures 6.1 and 6.2).

AUCTIONS

Sometimes plots are sold at auctions held by local estate agents and by large property practices specialising in such sales. The latter tend to deal with sales of land owned by bankrupt businesses and by other property-owning bodies. If you register with local estate agents they should tell you about any plots they are selling at auction; otherwise, look for auctions advertised in specialist property magazines - Estates Gazette and Property Week - and in local newspapers. An example of an auction notice is given in Figure 6.3.

PROPERTY PROFESSIONALS

Surveyors, building surveyors, architects, architectural technicians and planning consultants may know of plots coming up for sale either through their contacts in the property business, or through their work on specific sites. A telephone call to them could produce details of an ideal plot which is to be sold when planning permission is granted. Advance notice of such sites puts you well ahead of the competition and might mean you can buy before the plot ever comes onto the market.

LOCAL NETWORK

Use the local grapevine - family, friends, neighbours, colleagues and other contacts - to help you find a plot. Make sure everyone knows you are in the market to buy a building plot. They might know of someone with land for sale or with land that could make a suitable plot, or spot an advert or agents' board you have missed. Put up notices at your place of work, social clubs, pubs, church and anywhere else you can think of, saying that you are looking for a plot to build a house on. You can increase your chances of success dramatically by offering a reward for information that leads to the purchase of a site, perhaps £1,000. This might sound a lot but it is likely to be less than 1 per cent of your total cost and could easily make the difference between being able to build your own home or not.

LOCAL NEWSPAPERS

These are essential reading as they contain a wealth of useful information. Plots are advertised by estate agents or private individuals, listed under 'Houses for Sale', 'Land', 'Building Land' or 'Building Plots'. Local papers also have pages of houses for sale which give you an instant impression of the local housing market - what is available, price levels and which agents are active in particular areas. Scan the advertisements carefully, as plots can be hidden away among other properties, for example, 'Delightful Four bed Victorian house, living room, dining room, kitchen, garage, large orchard/possible building plot'. Some local papers list all local planning applications and Chapter 7 explains how to use this information.

Place your own advertisement in a local paper saying 'building plot wanted', stating whether you want a plot for a house or bungalow, and the area, and giving your telephone number. This could root out plots that might not otherwise come to light including ones owned by builders or vendors who, for various reasons, might not want to publicise their land for sale widely.

MAGAZINES

Look at specialist magazines catering for selfbuilders, particularly *Build It*, *Individual Homes: Homebuilding and Renovating* and *Selfbuild*, which advertise plots for sale. Plots are also advertised in papers like Exchange and Mart and Daltons Weekly and in the property pages of some national newspapers. As well as finding land, you can also see how many plots come up in your area, the level of asking prices and which agents are active in that area.

SELFBUILD PACKAGE COMPANIES

Selfbuild package companies give varying degrees help with land finding. If you are going to buy a house package from a particular company, obviously it will be anxious to help you in your plot search, as much as it can. Some have lists of building plots and/or names of agents and consultants who sell or find plots. Others give more active help and advice on plot buying. If you plan to buy a package, try speaking to a few companies and see what they can do for you.

BUILDERS MERCHANTS

The larger chains of builders merchants are increasingly gearing up to help selfbuilders and this includes efforts to help their potential customers to find land. Some maintain a register of plots on the market in their area, partly drawing on their contacts with local builders and tradesmen. Find out if the builders merchants in your area keep a plot list or what other help is available. A local builders merchant would also be a good place to leave a 'plot wanted' advertisement.

FIGURE 6.3 Front page of auction particulars

PARTICULARS AND CONDITIONS OF SALE

OF

OLD COPSE COTTAGE
Barn Lane, Tropton

A derelict Cottage with Outline Planning Permission
for demolition and replacement
Gardens and paddock, in all about 2.5 acres.

Freehold

FOR SALE BY AUCTION AS ONE LOT

Unless previously sold

by

Grimshaw, Hackett and Partners

At The Village Hall, Tropton, at 3.00pm,
Tuesday 12th April 1998

Solicitors:	Auction Offices:
Cantley, Grant and Thorn,	Grimshaw Hackett and Partners
Church Road,	High Street
Upchester	Upchester

FIGURE 6.4 Plot on a housing estate

Builders and developers building estates of houses are sometimes prepared to sell off plots to individuals. Look out for sites under construction like this one, where a couple of plots at the edge of the estate have been left undeveloped.

SHOWS AND EXHIBITIONS

Major selfbuild shows are held each year in Birmingham and London and smaller regional shows are held throughout the country. These are advertised in the selfbuild magazines. Plot finding services, selfbuild package companies and other useful organisations are represented. A chat with staff on the stands gives you an idea of what services they provide, about plot availability and the land market, and could provide you with some leads to follow up.

BUILDERS AND DEVELOPERS

Builders and developers sometimes own plots which they are prepared to sell, rather than build on themselves. Housing developers sometimes sell off individual plots in a larger scheme (see Figure 6.4). To protect their own interests they would probably want to vet the design of the house to be built. Other developers now cater specifically for selfbuilders: obtaining planning permission; sub-dividing the site; putting in access roads and services; and then selling individual plots.

A circular letter sent to local builders (addresses in Yellow Pages) might produce results. Be precise and brief in your letter. For example:

I am a cash buyer actively looking for a building plot in the Buckbridge/ Wingley area, and am ready to go ahead now. The plot must be suitable for a two storey, four bedroom house of about 1,700 square feet. If you have, or know of any suitable plots in the area, please telephone me on 123456 daytimes or 7891011 evenings.

In places where estate agents only sell plots to a few local builders you are effectively excluded from buying. If you come across this, and intend to use a builder to build your house anyway, say in your letter that you would retain the builder to do the work. This gives the builder extra incentive to sell to you, but you must find out about the cost and quality of their work before you commit yourself.

COUNCILS

Most district and borough councils own land in their areas, some of which can be suitable for building single houses. Telephone their estates departments to find out what is available. This varies between councils: where building land is scarce, there might be nothing; elsewhere, councils sometimes sell serviced plots specifically for selfbuilders. If you are interested in joining a selfbuild group, the council should be able to tell you about any that are forming locally. The Commission for the New Towns sells land, including single plots for individuals.

MAJOR LANDOWNERS

Large landowning bodies, like railway companies, the electricity, gas and water companies, breweries and British Telecom plc, sometimes sell surplus land suitable for house-building. Get the address of the estates department from your local branch or phone book and write or telephone with details of what you are looking for. Such organisations might sell through estate agents but you might, nevertheless, be able to get an early indication that a plot is coming up.

PLOT FINDING SERVICES

You might not have sufficient time available to search for plots yourself or you might have tried but failed to find the right piece of land; if so, consider getting help. There is a range of services available from specialist plot finding companies, estate agents and other companies. Look for these services advertised in the selfbuild magazines, or talk to the companies' staff at selfbuild shows.

If you are paying for help, there is a golden rule: get written confirmation of precisely what is going to be done, for how long, at what cost, and the circumstances in which you become liable for a fee or commission. Payment for plot-finding is often based on a commission - a percentage of the purchase price - paid either at exchange of contracts or completion. The percentage must be agreed at the outset and you should check whether out-of-pocket expenses are included. Alternatively, a fixed fee might be charged for the plot search or a fee based on the time taken. Beware of arrangements that seem open ended. You can be asked to pay a 'retainer' in advance of any work being done. Make sure you know whether this is refunded if no plot is found, or if it is deducted from the

FIGURE 6.5 List from computerised plot finding service

Ref	Location	Agent	Price £	Accom sq ft	Acreage
BLACKSHIRE					
317	Crompton Hatley	Private	35,000	1,200	.18
318	Akelfield	Private	60,000	1,600	.20
319	Hatstead	Brimptons	85,000	2,200	.34
320	Stockford	Holders	55,000	1,600	.18
321	Gunstock	A.G.	40,000	1,400	.12
322	Westley Wood	Brimptons	80.000	2,000	.51
323	Pinkton	Queens	60,000	1,600	.30
CRAMBOURNSHIRE					
414	Knockley	Private	30,000	1,800	.20
415	Plantry Common	Gollings	52,000	2,000	.23
416	High Wanstead	Smiths	75,000	2,500	.40
417	Woodcote	A.G.	25,000	1,500	.12
418	Tadfield	A.G.	60,000	2,200	.31
419	Stepton Green	Brimptons	50,000	1,800	.27

These lists give you just enough information to enable you to make a selection. Bear in mind that the prices are asking prices and the accommodation size probably a rough estimate only.

final fee or commission if you buy a plot.

Some services simply identify likely plots leaving you to do the rest, while others are more comprehensive, taking you through to completing the purchase. There are selfbuild packages that provide plot-finding as part of a service including site assessment, valuation, planning permission, purchase, Building Regulations and project management.

There are specialist companies offering computerised plot-finding services specifically for selfbuilders, such as Landbank Services (0118 9626022) which features a selection of its plots in *Build It* magazine, National Land Finding Agency (01371 876875) and the magazine *Individual Homes: Homebuilding and Renovating* which runs its own Plotfinder service. Generally, you subscribe on a quarterly basis and are sent lists of plots (see Figure 6.5) every week or month, taken from a database to which agents, local authorities and individuals contribute. This type of service is especially useful if you are searching for a plot a long way from your existing home, but because the land market often moves quickly, some entries can be out of date and the lists could include plots that agents are having trouble selling. On the other hand, some sites go only to land-finding agencies and so are only available to their subscribers. Apart from finding a plot directly, the computerised listings provide valuable market information - the areas in which plots are coming up, the level of asking prices and who handles the sale of plots in your area of search. Such market information alone is usually well worth the subscription.

With any type of plot-finding service, read the small print carefully as with some you can be liable to pay another fee if you buy a plot through the agency. Make sure you understand what sort of information or service you are going to be given.

Estate agents who sell land sometimes look for plots for clients as well; the sort of arrangement depends entirely on what you agree with them. Usually there is no fee unless you buy a plot that the agent finds for you, in which case you pay a commission or finder's fee of 1 or 2 per cent.

CHAPTER 7 HIDDEN OPPORTUNITIES

So far we have looked at finding building plots being offered for sale. Professional property developers do not wait for sites to be sold but adopt more direct methods. They seek out land with planning permission that has not been developed or look for suitable sites, see whether they can get planning permission and whether the owner will sell. There is nothing to stop you using the same methods.

PLANNING RECORDS

As building plots need planning permission, a good place to look is in the planning records. District, borough and city councils, or in metropolitan and a few other areas, unitary councils, deal with day-to-day planning matters in England. In Scotland they are dealt with by the councils, in Wales by county or county borough councils and in Northern Ireland by the divisional offices of the Department of the Environment Town and Country Planning Service. For convenience we will use the term 'district council' throughout this book to cover all of these. District councils keep records in their planning departments of all past and present planning applications which are available for public inspection. You can find out if a particular piece of land has planning permission or if an application has been refused in the past. You should look for plots with planning permission that have not been built on, which you hope the owner will sell.

The first step is to check the records for what planning permissions exist. District councils' record systems vary, as does their enthusiasm for delving into them. Looking up planning records can occupy an enjoyable ten minutes or several frustrating hours. Since searching through the records of a whole area

would take a long time, concentrate on one town or parish at a time. An actual address or, better still, a planning application reference number, speeds things up, but you do not need to know who owns the site to look up the records. There is a record of every planning permission, often listed by parish or other area. Go back over these and make a note of all permissions for houses, including the name and address of the person who made the application. Some district councils also mark the reference number of all planning applications on Ordnance Survey maps, making it easy to see where applications have been made, but not what the applications were actually for. Study the maps to identify likely sites where an application has been made and write down the reference number and address. Look up the application or ask for the planning record card of the property, which sets out its history of applications.

Some permissions will not be for the right type of house, or in the right place; others, you might know, have already been built. Any remaining sites should be checked by a visit to see if work has started.

District councils produce a list of the planning applications made each week which you can see at their offices, at parish council offices, local libraries or listed in a local newspaper. This list gives the reference, type of application and address, for example, 'R/98/1648, outline, single detached dwelling and double garage, Mill Lane, Riverton'. You can ask at the planning department to see the application which contains useful information, including the size and location of the plot, and who owns it.

An application made in outline is generally a better bet than a detailed

FIGURE 7.1 Local Plan insert map

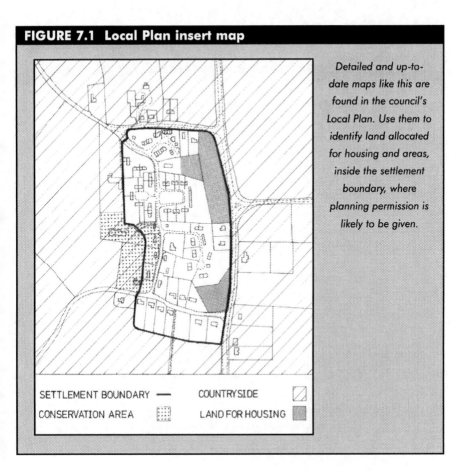

Detailed and up-to-date maps like this are found in the council's Local Plan. Use them to identify land allocated for housing and areas, inside the settlement boundary, where planning permission is likely to be given.

SETTLEMENT BOUNDARY ——   COUNTRYSIDE ▨

CONSERVATION AREA ⬚   LAND FOR HOUSING ▨

application, as outline is often used to establish the principle that a house can be built on the plot before it is sold. A detailed application can mean that the scheme is farther advanced and that either the owner is going to build or has a buyer already. In some situations, for example, in Conservation Areas, district councils are likely to require all applications to be made in detail. So, if an application alerts you to a suitable plot, pursue it regardless of the type of application involved.

LOCAL PLANS

District councils draw up Local Plans containing planning policies for development in their areas. Some districts have more than one plan, but all are now working towards a single plan for their entire area. The system of plans is complex and Local Plans are sometimes confused with Structure Plans prepared by county councils which set out more general planning policies for a county or region. Often terms are used such as 'local structure plan' or 'village development plan'

FIGURE 7.2 Local Plan policies

◆ **Typical Local Plan policy applying to new housing in the countryside**

Outside the defined built up areas there will be a strong presumption against proposals for new housing development. Exceptions may be made for dwellings for agriculture or forestry workers where there is a proven and overriding need, subject to the detailed criteria laid down in Policy AG4.

◆ **Typical Local Plan policy for new housing within a settlement**

Within the defined settlement boundaries, planning permission will normally be granted for proposals for residential development, only if the following criteria are met:

1. The land is not allocated for some other purpose in the Local Plan.
2. The scale, density and form of the proposed development reflects that of the general locality.
3. The new dwelling plots formed would not be significantly smaller than the average for those in the neighbourhood.
4. The provision for car parking and vehicle manoeuvring does not significantly reduce garden areas or adversely affect adjoining property.
5. The adjoining highways have the capacity to accommodate the additional traffic generated by the development.
6. Other normal development control criteria can be met.

which are technically meaningless (but can be useful nevertheless as they betray the users' fragile understanding of the subtleties of the planning system).

There is a slightly different type of plan used in Wales, in metropolitan areas (Greater London, Greater Manchester, Merseyside, South Yorkshire, Tyne and Wear, West Midlands and West Yorkshire) and by just a few other English councils. Here Structure and Local Plans are combined into one document called a Unitary Development Plan.

Local Plans consist of a proposals map showing the area, and a written document

(see Figures 7.1 and 7.2). Some areas, like town centres, are shown in detail on inset maps either bound in the written document or on separate sheets with the main proposals map.

Local Plans usually distinguish between 'settlements' and 'countryside'. Settlements are towns, villages and perhaps small hamlets. Around each settlement a line is drawn on the proposals map (see Figure 7.1), which is known variously as the 'Settlement Boundary', 'Built Up Area Boundary', 'Housing Framework' or 'Village Envelope', but all mean the same. Beyond this line,

Hidden Opportunities

restrictive policies apply which mean that opportunities for building on greenfield sites in the countryside are very few and far between. On the other hand, policies inside settlement boundaries allow new houses to be built in residential areas and sites for new housing estates are shown. Settlement boundaries do not always follow obvious lines: the outskirts of towns and villages can be excluded and so be considered 'countryside' in planning terms.

Local Plans show Conservation Areas, Green Belts, Areas of Outstanding Natural Beauty (AONB), or National Scenic Areas in Scotland, and other specially designated areas. All these designations restrict the type of development that can take place within their boundaries.

Look at the Local Plan covering your area of search at the district council's offices or at a local library. Study the proposals map to identify likely sites or areas where there might be plots. You can then research the planning history of the site or area, in the way described in the previous section, to find if planning permission has been granted and who owns the land. Use the Local Plan if you find a potential plot without planning permission; look it up on the proposals map to see whether it comes in an area where development is allowed. The companion to this book, **How to Get Planning Permission**, has more detail on planning applications, appeals and Local Plans (see page 3).

ORDNANCE SURVEY MAPS

If you are determined to build in one particular area, say a small village, obtain the Ordnance Survey map or maps that cover it. Ordnance Survey maps at 1:2,500 or 1:1,250 scale show individual houses, gardens and pieces of land, enabling you to identify potential plots. Figure 7.3 shows the amount of detail the maps give. You can buy them from local Ordnance Survey agents, whose addresses are in Yellow Pages. Each map only covers a relatively small area and they are expensive. Libraries also keep copies of local Ordnance Survey maps. Check the date of the map, in some areas even the most up-to-date are over ten years old and much could have changed in that time.

IDENTIFYING POTENTIAL PLOTS ON THE GROUND

Local Plans and Ordnance Survey maps might help identify likely places to find plots, but also explore your area of search by car, bicycle or on foot. Look for things like gaps in an otherwise built-up road frontage, houses with large gardens that could be sub-divided, and extra long or extra wide plots. Figure 7.4 gives an idea of the opportunities. Plots can be created by combining land in two or more different ownerships, and trees, hedges, sheds and garages can obscure potential plots, so you need imagination. Look for adequately sized pieces of land, especially frontages. Check whether it is possible for access from the plot to the road to be arranged. Envisage where a house could be sited on the plot and whether this would fit in with the surroundings or affect the privacy of other existing houses. If so, see whether these problems could be overcome by siting the house in a different place, by a clever design or by landscaping. These preliminary questions determine whether you have a possible plot to investigate further.

A word here about so called 'backland' and 'tandem' development. This is where a

FIGURE 7.3 Ordnance Survey map

Use Ordnance Survey maps to find possible plots - rear gardens, side gardens, vacant sites. Bear in mind where planning policy boundaries lie, because outside the council's settlement boundary getting planning permission is much harder. The settlement boundary and potential plots have been drawn onto this representation of an Ordnance Survey map.

POSSIBLE PLOTS

LOCAL PLAN SETTLEMENT BOUNDARY

large back garden is sub-divided to create a plot, often with an access drive running past the existing house and down the side of its garden to the plot. Backland development is not satisfactory where existing properties would lose their privacy, or where there would be noise and disturbance from the use of a new drive. It is sometimes possible for houses on backland plots to be designed so that these problems do not occur. Most district councils' planning officers are against backland development as a matter of principle, regardless of the merits of the case, and so

applications are turned down which might be granted planning permission at appeal. In some areas, backland development is an established part of the local pattern of building, so do not dismiss these sites. They can make ideal plots, especially if you are looking for a quiet spot away from a road.

THE PLOT IN YOUR GARDEN

Many selfbuilders build in the garden of their own home, so do not overlook possibilities on your doorstep (see Figure 7.5). If there is not enough space, think about buying-in other

Hidden Opportunities

land to make a plot. Beyond this, look for houses on the market that have a plot, or potential plot, in the garden. You can buy the house and either sell it straight away, just keeping the plot, or live in it while you build, and then sell. There could be some sobering cash flow implications in such an arrangement. There are advantages to building in your own garden. Your new home design is less likely to be limited by covenants; access, drainage and fencing can be easier to arrange; and you can live on the site to supervise and monitor the build in comfort. There is plenty of scope to profit from creating your own plot, but profit is closely linked to risk. If you buy a house and plot with planning permission, you will probably pay the full market price for both. If you buy a house with a large garden with potential, you will run the risk of being refused planning permission.

SUB-STANDARD PROPERTY

Sub-standard houses and buildings sometimes provide opportunities for demolition and rebuilding which have to be identified on the ground as maps make no distinction between sound and derelict buildings. Local planning policies on replacement houses, and how they are interpreted, vary between district councils. Ask a planning officer how applications for replacement houses are dealt with locally.

Remember, planning policies are different for settlements and countryside. Policies often limit the size of replacement houses in the countryside, but through clever design you might be able to come up with a building which looks less conspicuous than the original, but which is actually larger. If the sub-standard building is a pair of semi-detached houses, there is more scope for

justifying an increased floor area. The reduced activity generated by one dwelling, as opposed to two, is offset against the increase in size of building.

There might be cost savings with demolition and re-building where the existing access, services and/or service connections, landscaping or salvageable building materials can be used.

CONVERSIONS

Many buildings lend themselves to conversion into houses - barns, stables, schools, churches, workshops - even water towers and public loos have been converted. Much of the guidance in this book applies equally to finding and buying conversion properties. Most properties for conversion are sold by estate agents, but also look for opportunities by driving around the area. Depending on the quality, stability and layout of the existing building, conversion can cost more or less than starting with a clear site.

Converting barns and rural buildings gives wider scope for creating new homes in the countryside. Government planning guidelines now say that the appearance and character of rural buildings is usually better preserved by conversion to commercial, industrial or recreational uses, rather than houses. Local policies vary, but generally speaking it is easier to get planning permission to convert a rural building in a village or hamlet than for one that is isolated or on a farm.

FINDING THE OWNER

Once you have located a potential plot, you need to find the owner. Of course, if you are out and about plot-hunting you could simply ask at the nearest house or in the local pub,

FIGURE 7.4 Identifying potential plots

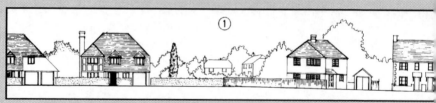

Look in your chosen location for opportunities to create plots, e.g. (1) combining side gardens, (2) demolishing old buildings, (3) orchards, paddocks or large gardens.

FIGURE 7.5 Back garden plot

Some people are lucky enough to have a potential plot in their own garden which they can build on or sell off. Planning policies, access, ground conditions and covenants still have to be checked. Councils have an aversion to allowing new houses to be built behind others, regardless of how well they fit in.

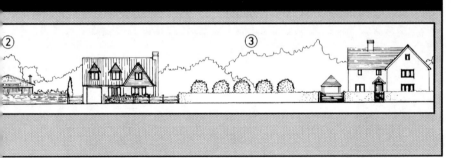

shop or post office. If the plot has a planning history, you can get details of ownership from previous planning applications at the district council's offices. Old rating and community charge records at the council's offices might also help. If you have an address, get the name of the occupier from the electoral roll at a local library. The occupier is likely to own the property, but could instead be a tenant who can give you the owner's name. If it is not obvious which property the potential plot belongs to, get the names of a few neighbours from the electoral roll and write or telephone to find out if they know who owns it.

You can get details of properties from the Land Registry, where the ownership, or title, has been registered; registration is now compulsory whenever properties change hands. Land that has been in the same ownership for many years is unlikely to be registered. If the land is registered you can get information on ownership and restrictions, such as restrictive covenants, mortgages, leases or rights of way, and a title plan which is an Ordnance Survey map marked with the boundaries of the registered title. A small charge is made for inspecting and getting copies from the register. You can obtain information from the Land Registry either by

post or by calling-in to inspect the register. If calling-in, it is worth telephoning first and giving the address of the property you want to look up, as this avoids having to wait while the documents are found when you arrive. When writing, you must give an address or identify the property on an Ordnance Survey map and you also need to enclose a cheque - telephone to find out current fees. The ownership information should be sent back within about four days. The Land Registry is a user-friendly organisation, so if you are uncertain about how to use the service, give the staff a call. Your nearest Land Registry office does not necessarily deal with your area; for example, the office covering Surrey is in Durham. For more information contact: HM Land Registry, 32 Lincoln's Inn Fields, London WC2A 3PH (0171 9178888).

When you have the name and address, write to the owner. What you say depends partly on how you have found the plot - through a new planning application, an existing permission, or by spotting an opportunity. Say you are interested in buying the plot and ask whether the owner intends to sell or would be prepared to consider it. If you are lucky and the plot is to be sold, you will at worst be ahead of the competition; at best the

FIGURE 7.6 House for replacement

While searching for land to build on, do not overlook opportunities to demolish small properties, especially in the countryside where houses on new sites would not be allowed.

vendor might dispense with the time and cost of marketing through an agent and sell direct to you.

AGRICULTURAL DWELLINGS

In very limited circumstances it is possible to build a new farmhouse or agricultural worker's cottage in the countryside where an existing agricultural business needs someone on site day and night and there is no alternative accommodation nearby. This does not mean you can buy an acre of agricultural land and a few chickens, call it a farm and get planning permission to build a house. District councils,

backed by government advice, apply stringent tests to all applications. Even in genuine cases of agricultural need, councils often only give a temporary planning permission for a mobile home, which has to be renewed, or upgraded to a house after two or three years when the need has been established beyond all reasonable doubt. These houses are subject to an 'agricultural tie' limiting who can occupy the house; we look at this in more detail in Chapter 12. If you think you have a case to justify an agricultural dwelling, get specialist professional advice from a planning consultant.

FIGURE 7.7 Barn conversion

Existing buildings, including farm buildings, offer scope for creating individual homes with plenty of character, often in places where planning permission for a new house would not be given. Councils expect conversions to respect the appearance of traditional buildings which can affect the practicality of internal layouts.

FINDING THE PLOT - CHECK LIST

- ◆ Register with local estate agents.
- ◆ Read classified adverts in local papers and put a 'building plot wanted' advert in local papers.
- ◆ Find out about plot-finding services
- ◆ Ask your building designer, selfbuild package company, or builder, for help and information about plots.
- ◆ Check whether councils in the area or other authorities sell single plots.
- ◆ Write to local builders or housing developers.
- ◆ Speak to property professionals - surveyors, architects, and technicians.
- ◆ Look at councils' Local Plans and planning records.
- ◆ Study maps and look on the ground to identify potential plots and write to owners.

Once you find what looks like the right plot, you have to be sure you can build the home you want on it. There are factors which can stop you doing this - some could rule out building altogether, others could dictate every detail of what and where you can build. You can check most aspects of your plot quite easily, but some points are not obvious and others need much investigation.

To avoid costly mistakes, you must discover anything that might inhibit or add cost to the building of your house, before you agree a price or commit yourself to buying the plot. In this Part we show you step-by-step how to assess your plot, point out pitfalls you might encounter and tell you ways to overcome them.

The first points to consider are the physical features of a plot; most of these can be assessed by looking at the site, but there are those that need investigation.

FITTING THE HOUSE ON THE PLOT

Check that the home you want to build will actually fit the plot, taking account of restrictions and neighbouring houses. With rectangular plots, it is usually a simple matter of whether the frontage is adequate for the width of the house and garage. Where a plot is of an irregular shape, get a scale plan, which can be an Ordnance Survey extract taken from agents' particulars or a planning permission and enlarged on a photocopier. Draw and cut out outlines of the ground-floor plan of the house and garage to the same scale, and move them around the site plan to find the best layout. If you have trouble fitting them on the plot try 'handing' the house, that is making it a mirror image of the original layout by turning your cut-out floor plan over and placing it face down. This can help to solve problems caused by overlooking other houses or gardens next to the plot or make the most of sunlight in main rooms of the house.

Where space is limited, take check measurements on site, as site plans' measurements given on application drawings and agents' particulars are often inaccurate. An error of only one metre in the plot frontage could mean that your dream home simply will not fit on the plot.

THE LIE OF THE LAND

Look at the lie of the land within the plot and in relation to the land around. Steep slopes add to build costs of the house, drive and landscaping. Earth-moving and levelling is expensive and can spoil natural contours, possibly jeopardising planning permission. If the plot is low-lying, consider the risk of flooding and whether floors would have to be set at a high level, again increasing building cost. If the plot is on high ground or in an exposed position, consider the prevailing wind and the access - a plot on a steep hill could become inaccessible in snow or icy weather.

Find out if a site survey, showing levels, has been done. For plots with a steep slope you will need a survey at some point to make sure that the scheme works. A site survey is also useful to pinpoint trees, vegetation and boundaries and in making planning and Building Regulations applications. Use your building designer to carry out a survey for you, or contact a land surveyor; you will find these in Yellow Pages under 'Surveyors - Land'.

GROUND CONDITIONS

Wet or unstable ground could increase the cost of foundations. When inspecting a site in dry weather, check for areas which might be wet in winter by looking at the plant life. Clumps of reeds or rushes and willow or alder trees indicate wet ground, or possibly a spring. A line of willow or alder across a site can mark the course of an underground stream. Some areas are prone to subsidence because of mining or geological faults; look for signs like cracks, sunken areas and holes. Examples of what to look for are given in Figures 8.1, 8.2 and 8.3.

Look at old maps in the local library to find out about past uses of the land. Some sites comprise made-up ground, such as old clay pits or village ponds which have been filled over the years. Former industrial land might be contaminated, for example, old gas-holder sites, scrapyards or chemical works.

Contaminated ground can be dangerous and cleaning-up costs high.

The type of soil influences the design and cost of foundations. Heavy clay and soft sand are common soil types that necessitate careful choice of foundations. Foundations can be designed to cope with poor ground conditions and in some cases the ground itself can be consolidated prior to building. The cost of special foundations might be only marginally higher than standard foundations. But, if your budget is very tight, poor ground conditions could mean looking for a different plot.

Speak to an officer of the building control section at the district council who can give you an idea of all likely ground condition problems found in the area. If you are concerned about ground conditions, have a site investigation carried out by a builder, building surveyor or soil engineer. Ask your building designer who to use or look up 'Site Investigations' in Yellow Pages.

TREES AND VEGETATION

Trees and other vegetation, like shrubs, bushes and hedges, can both help and hinder your development of a plot and so must be taken into account at an early stage. Trees are often a constraint when positioning a house on a plot, as building is usually not allowed closer to a tree than two-thirds of its mature height. District councils generally expect you to keep as many trees as possible, especially individual specimen trees and attractive groups, and can make Tree Preservation Orders, which we look at in Chapter 12.

Trees can affect the foundations of buildings, especially on shrinkable clay, where

FIGURE 8.1 Constraints to building

Many factors can affect where and how you build on a plot. Illustrated in this drawing are the position and outlook of nearby houses; overhead cables; sewers (manhole covers); footpath; wet ground; tipping; and trees.

A careful inspection of a plot will reveal most constraints to building which you should look into. Made-up ground and wet ground shown in the top photograph need further investigation into possible clean-up costs, drainage or special foundations. Trees and a well trodden path must be checked in the council's records of protected trees, and on the definitive footpath map or with your solicitor.

their roots dry out the soil, causing shrinkage and possibly subsidence. If trees are felled, the soil can swell subsequently. Trees with the highest water demand are elm, oak, poplar and willow.

Trees and shrubs benefit plots by providing an instant mature setting, creating privacy between neighbours and acting as a wind-break, all of which can add to the value of your finished home. They can, however, cut out light or block views.

Mark on a plan the position, spread of the branches, and species of all trees on and next to the plot, and any recently cut down. If you have a site survey, ask for these details to be included. Take account of this information when working out how your house would fit the plot and use it later in making a planning application and getting foundations designed.

OBSTACLES

Obstacles like telegraph poles, manhole covers or wellshafts can affect site layout and cost of the build. Manhole covers might indicate the existence of a main sewer and you cannot generally build within 3 m (10 ft) of a sewer, but this sometimes varies according to its size and depth. Sewers can be diverted, assuming that an adequate gradient can be maintained, and how much this will cost depends on the distance, size and depth of sewer and the number of new manholes needed. If you cannot avoid building over the line of a sewer, get quotes for the cost of having it moved. Telegraph poles and electricity supply lines can be subject to rights (or easements) which allow the service company onto the site for maintenance purposes. If there are any service supply pipes, cables or apparatus on the plot, ask your solicitor to check carefully for rights

attached to them. You can have telegraph and electricity poles moved; contact the service companies about this.

If there are buildings on the plot, bear in mind the cost of demolition, including digging out foundations which might be all that is left, but not visible. Cost depends on the type of building - a dilapidated shed would cost next to nothing to remove, but a World War Two bunker could cost a fortune. Get quotes from demolition contractors. You must obtain permission from the district council to demolish buildings in a Conservation Area.

ORIENTATION

Check the orientation of the plot - north, south, east or west - as this influences the amount of sun and shade in house and garden. Look at this in relation to trees and neighbouring properties that could cast shadows in your garden. Remember that, if you want to build energy efficiency into your home, a southerly aspect makes the most of the sun's heat and light. When considering orientation, also check the direction of prevailing winds which can have a bearing on the design of your house, as it is better for main doors to be sheltered.

BOUNDARIES

Check the boundaries to be clear about what is included in the plot you are buying. Ask the vendor, or his agent, for a copy of the plan from the title deeds which shows the boundaries of legal ownership. Old deed plans are often based on out-of-date maps and boundary lines may be drawn so thickly that their precise position is open to argument. Fences and hedges do not always coincide with legal ownership boundaries. If a boundary is not clear, speak to the vendor first, and possibly to the neighbours, to clarify the position. Avoid boundary disputes as they can be costly and time consuming. Where a boundary is disputed, get an accurate site survey drawing to form the basis for agreeing a solution. Ordnance Survey plans show where there are physical boundaries, but not who owns them. The district council cannot help in any boundary disputes, unless they happen to own the adjacent land. Lines marked on previous planning application plans give guidance, but have no legal status.

Where the boundary is just a hedge, the centre line is usually taken as the legal boundary. Where there is a hedge and a ditch, the edge of the ditch farthest from the hedge is generally the legal boundary. It is assumed that a land owner first digs the ditch along his boundary and then plants the hedge on his own land, on top of the excavated soil.

ADJOINING USES

When assessing your plot it is also important to check adjoining land uses and the wider surroundings for anything that could spoil your enjoyment of the property and whether the situation could change. Investigate building works of any kind or vacant land with development potential, or commission a Planning Search (see page 159). Make a note of any areas which you think might be vulnerable to undesirable change so that you can look into them at the planning department of the district council.

If your first look at a plot was at a weekend, go back and look for schools, businesses or industry that create noise, smells or traffic during the week, especially if they are upwind from your plot. In rural areas consider what it would be like to live downwind from a chicken farm or abattoir. How ever well you know the area, find your plot on the Local Plan proposals map, which you can see either at the district council or at a local library. This will give you an insight into how the area is planned to develop in future.

It is always worth finding out why a plot has not been built on before, especially if it has been on the market for some time. Ask the vendor or selling agent; there is often a good reason but there might be some physical or legal problem which has inhibited building on the plot. If you are at all suspicious, tell your solicitor and be vigilant when checking all the points covered in this part of the book.

THE PROPERTY MARKET

At first sight, the current state of the property market might not seem relevant to your assessment of a plot, but it can be. Assessing a plot properly takes time and can cost you money. In a busy plot market there might not be time to research everything as thoroughly as you would like before exchanging contracts, so you need to concentrate on those things that could prevent you building altogether, or could add substantial cost. In a slow property market, where vendors can be desperate to sell, you should be able to load more of the time and cost of assessment on to the vendor and his agent.

A building plot needs vehicular access to a public highway which meets highway safety standards. In almost all cases, this is straightforward, as part of the plot usually fronts on to a road, and a new or existing opening is used to build an access and driveway. There is sometimes more to the question of access than first meets the eye and failure to provide adequate access can mean failure to build a house. There are two separate aspects to consider; one is the legal right of access to a road, and the other is complying with highway authority standards.

These are completely separate matters and both must be satisfied.

A new access comprises: a kerb; a crossover (the section of drive that crosses the verge and any footpath) and the drive itself; and usually an on-site turning area for vehicles. Accesses can be single, shared or paired (see Figure 9.1). A shared access is a single drive serving two or more houses. A paired access is where two access points come together at the road frontage creating a double width crossover which is shared between the two properties. A paired access is

FIGURE 9.1 Examples of accesses and drives

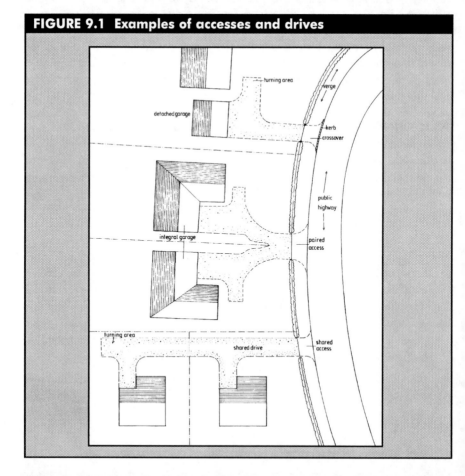

usually used where there is not enough space in each plot to comply with highway authority standards.

Most roads are public adopted highways which means that they are owned and maintained by a local highway authority - in England this is normally the county council or, in metropolitan and other single-tier authority areas, the council; in Scotland, the council; in Wales, the county or county borough council; and in Northern Ireland, the Roads Service of the Department of the Environment. Roads are classified A, B or C; very small roads and estate roads are unclassified. Finally, there are unadopted and private roads. New accesses directly onto motorways and trunk roads are not permitted.

LEGAL CONSIDERATIONS

When you have planning permission to build a house, and your plot adjoins a public road, you do not need separate permission to get access. Where access from a plot would be onto an unadopted or private road, check that there is a right to use that road and who is responsible for its maintenance. Surprisingly, there is often no clear answer and, in these cases, residents whose properties front the private road sometimes group together to share maintenance costs. Alternatively, residents ask the highway authority to adopt the road which they will generally do only if the road is built to its standards. Making up a road to the required standard can be very expensive, or impossible if the existing road is too narrow and residents are unwilling to lose strips of their front gardens. Where the precise ownership of a road cannot be discovered, you can take out insurance cover against a challenge to your right to use the road in future. Different ownerships of sections of road are often obvious on the ground because of changes in surfacing; beware of a neat tarmac road that gives way to hardcore and potholes just short of the plot.

VERGES

Another area where land ownership is often unclear is at the roadside verge. In most cases, where a plot fronts a road, land between the edge of the road and a plot boundary is owned and maintained by the local highway authority. This might be grass verge or pavement and you are allowed to cross it without having to pay for a right.

COMMON LAND

The access to a plot could run over common land, which could be in one ownership but subject to various rights granted to other people. Although these might be of the 'right to graze three pigs and a gaggle of geese between the months of July and October' variety, they can still prevent you getting access.

RANSOM STRIPS

Where there is land in somebody else's ownership between your land and the public highway there could be a ransom strip (see Figure 9.2). There is no automatic right to cross such land unless you get, or the plot already has, a specific right of access. A ransom strip can be a few inches wide, but in such a case an inch is as good as a mile. The owner of the ransom strip in effect controls whether or not you can build on your plot, and hence the 'ransom'. Ransoms often exist where the roadside verge is in another ownership which might be the parish or district council or a private individual. It could even be owned by the council that is the

FIGURE 9.2 Ransom strips

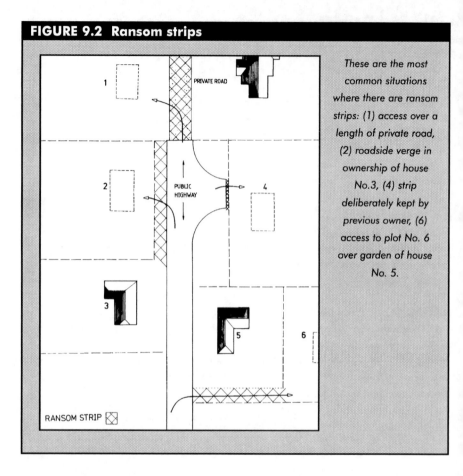

These are the most common situations where there are ransom strips: (1) access over a length of private road, (2) roadside verge in ownership of house No.3, (4) strip deliberately kept by previous owner, (6) access to plot No. 6 over garden of house No. 5.

highway authority, but not be part of the public highway, and so there is no automatic right to cross it.

It is your solicitors' job to check that you can get access to the plot and their normal investigations during your purchase should show up any defects or problems. Make sure your solicitors' searches include not just the plot itself but also a strip of access road outside it. If you find there is difficulty over access, normally leave it to the vendor to sort out and do not buy the plot until it is resolved.

Overcoming a ransom strip usually means buying the land in question or a right of access over it, but there is nothing to say that an owner has to sell. Anyone who realises the importance of the ransom strip will probably want some of the development value of the plot. Development value means what the land is worth as a building plot, less its value for its existing use as garden or field. In a well known legal case, Stokes v. Cambridge (1961), a third of the development value was paid for an access. The amount of ransom money paid is a matter for negotiation and depends on whether there are alternative ways to get access. Buying a ransom strip should not, however, affect the overall price you pay for a plot. Either the vendor pays the ransom or if you have to pay, say a £10,000 ransom for access, then you reduce your bid for the plot by £10,000. If a ransom strip has to be bought out, your solicitors might need the backing of a surveyor or valuer to provide valuations. If the owner of the ransom refuses to sell, your only option is to find a different plot.

HIGHWAY STANDARDS

Highway authority standards concern: visibility at the point of access onto the highway; construction of the kerb and crossover; width and length of the drive; and parking and turning facilities. Highway standards are applied and assessed when planning applications are made for new houses. The highway authority comments on access and turning arrangements and sets out its requirements which the district council can include in a condition when giving planning permission. So, where planning permission has already been given, assuming that you can comply with any highway conditions attached to it (and subject to having the necessary legal rights), then you can go ahead and build the access. If the plot does not have planning permission, check that you can meet highway standards.

There must be clear visibility at the point of access onto the highway so that approaching drivers can see an emerging vehicle, and vice versa. This can rule out new accesses near sharp bends, near the crest of a hill or where there are double white lines in the centre of the road, indicating that forward visibility is poor.

There must be a visibility splay at each side of an access, that is areas that must be kept free of obstructions so that lines of sight are clear (see Figure 9.3). The drive of a single house usually requires a clear view up and down the road from a point 2.4 m (8 ft) back from the edge of the road. In urban areas with 30 miles-per-hour speed limits, this point can be a minimum of 2 m (6ft 6ins). The distance for which a driver must be able to see along the road varies according to the type of road and speed of traffic. It can be as little as 33 m (110 ft) in each direction, where traffic is very slow moving, and more than 200 m (666 ft) where traffic is fast moving.

Check visibility by taking two-and-a-half paces back from the edge of road, at the centre of the access point, and look up and down the road. A neighbour's hedge or fence could block the view, or a tree, telegraph pole, road sign or bus shelter might be in just the wrong spot. Where visibility is blocked, find out who owns the hedge, fence or obstruction, and whether you can have it moved and at what cost. An obstruction which prevents adequate visibility can jeopardise planning permission, and an astute owner could hold you to ransom. Do not assume that street trees can necessarily be felled or cut back, they may be protected by a TPO. If bus shelters, pillar boxes or telegraph poles must be moved, you will have to pay the cost. Before you decide to buy a plot, make sure you know what any such costs would be.

Parking and turning standards vary according to the size of house and type of road. As a general rule, there must be sufficient turning space on site so that cars do not have to back out onto the road. If your drive is long, you might need a lorry-turning area so that fire engines or dustcarts can enter and turn around.

Note, at this stage, that building regulations permission can be refused where fire engines cannot get access to a house with a long drive. This could stop you building, even though planning permission might have been given.

Where you cannot comply with highway standards, and highway safety would be threatened as a result, the district council is likely to refuse planning permission. Highway standards are not always rigidly applied and, if your scheme is acceptable in all other respects, there might be some flexibility, although planning applications are often refused for access and highway safety reasons. If you have trouble, get professional advice from a planning consultant or highway engineer.

FIGURE 9.3 Visibility for an access drive

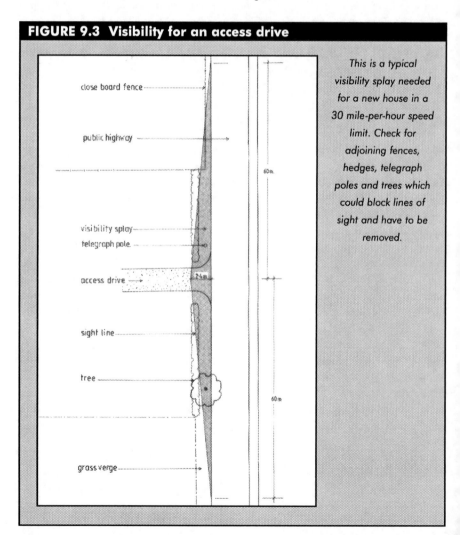

This is a typical visibility splay needed for a new house in a 30 mile-per-hour speed limit. Check for adjoining fences, hedges, telegraph poles and trees which could block lines of sight and have to be removed.

Investigate services at an early stage in your assessment of a plot, not as an afterthought when you have bought it. Look into the availability and cost of connection to the main services: drainage, water, electricity, gas and telephone. Where main services are not available, you should explore alternatives. Foul and surface water drainage has to be approved by the district council, which can refuse planning permission for a new house if the proposed drainage is not satisfactory. Services running under or over a site can be an obstacle to building, so you also need to find out their locations for this reason.

FOUL DRAINAGE

The first choice for foul drainage is usually a connection to the nearest public foul sewer. Sewer records, based on Ordnance Survey maps, showing the position, depth and size of drains are kept either by the drainage authority or by the district council (see Figure 10.1). Levels at manholes are marked on the record including a cover level (top of the manhole cover) and an invert level (bottom of the sewer pipe) and the difference between the two gives the depth of the sewer. Visit the drainage authority's offices to look at the record or write to the authority and ask where the nearest sewer is and whether you can connect to it.

Connection to a public foul sewer can usually be made where there is a fall in level from house to sewer, and the sewer has adequate capacity. If the sewer is uphill, a pump system can be used which might increase cost but now, with the development of small bore systems, pumping is more viable. While investigating sewers check on connection charges and take account of the distance to the sewer and whether you have to cross a road to it as these factors add to the cost. Sometimes a public foul sewer can only be reached by crossing someone else's land or connection has to be made via a private sewer. In either case, the necessary rights have to be negotiated with and acquired from the owner in order to make a connection.

In some areas, when you apply for planning permission for a new house, you will meet a drainage embargo which stops you connecting into the public sewers because the drains or the sewage treatment plant have reached capacity and need replacing or upgrading. If a plot is affected by a drainage embargo, talk to the drainage authority and district council to find out how long it might last and whether there is a way of getting around it.

Where there is no public sewer available, investigate private disposal systems - septic tank, sealed cesspool or private treatment plant. A septic tank is a large container, sunk into the ground usually at least 15 m (50 ft) from the house, which needs emptying about once a year. Septic tanks require an area of land, well away from the house, into which the treated water drains and, if the plot itself is not large enough, you would need to negotiate the use of some adjoining land. You must get approval for a septic tank from the Environment Agency in England and Wales, the Rivers Purification Boards in Scotland or the Water Service of the Department of the Environment in Northern Ireland. In areas of impervious clay, where there is a high ground water table or where there is a river or stream nearby, a septic tank might not be allowed.

The modern alternative to a septic tank is a mini treatment plant and a number of different models are made, suitable to serve individual houses. Unlike a septic tank, the water discharged can usually go direct into a

FIGURE 10.1 Example record of public sewers

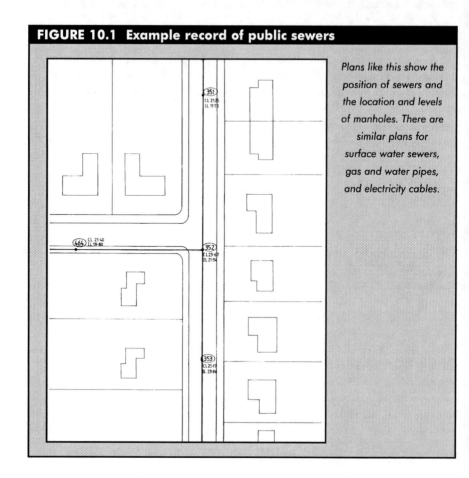

Plans like this show the position of sewers and the location and levels of manholes. There are similar plans for surface water sewers, gas and water pipes, and electricity cables.

watercourse but check with the Environment Agency, Rivers Purification Board or Water Service whether these systems are allowed in your area.

A cesspool is simply a large sealed tank that has to be emptied six to twelve times a year by tanker for which you need to provide access. Look into the likely cost of emptying, especially in remote areas.

SURFACE WATER DRAINAGE

Surface water drainage takes care of the water from the roofs of the house and garage

and possibly from drives and other hard surfaces. Soakaways are commonly used to disperse surface water and consist of a large pit filled with rubble from which surface water seeps into the surrounding soil. The size and number of soakaways you will need varies with the size of house and type of soil. In areas where the soil is impervious or the water table is high, soakaways are not permitted or are only allowed after percolation tests have been carried out. Speak to the building control section of the district council about surface water drainage, as they know the local ground conditions and can tell you about likely difficulties.

If your plot is next to, or crossed by, a ditch or stream, a piped outfall discharging surface water directly into it might be permitted. In areas liable to flood or where you build as part of a group of houses, you can be asked to provide flood prevention measures, like a holding tank to take the first rush of water after a downpour. In urban areas there are sometimes public surface water sewers into which you can connect and, in very limited cases, you are allowed to connect to the public foul sewer. Road drains are not public surface water sewers and you need the highway authority's permission to connect to them. As with foul sewers, if you have to cross someone else's land to make a connection you will probably have to pay.

WATER

The local water company has records of the position and size of water mains. These usually follow roads and in most cases are readily available but check connection charges as they can be high. Where a water main is not available, ask the water company about the cost of laying a supply to your property. They are obliged to do this, but you

have to contribute to the cost which, if the nearest main is miles away, is likely to be prohibitive. In those circumstances speak to the local water company about alternative water sources, like bore holes, streams and springs, and whether you need an abstraction licence. Find out the cost of putting in and running a private system.

OTHER SERVICES

Mains electricity is widely available, gas less so. The gas and electricity supply companies can give you details of the nearest supply and tell you whether a connection can be made and at what cost. If mains gas is not available, bulk storage tanks are an alternative.

If you want to use oil, this also needs a storage tank. Decide where these could be put on a plot and how you would get access for refilling. If possible, position tanks so that they can be filled by a hose, while the delivery tanker stays on the road, as not all private drives can take the weight of a fully laden lorry.

In remote areas the cost of a telephone connection can be high if there are no existing lines nearby. Check the likely cost with British Telecom plc if you cannot see telephone lines anywhere near the plot.

A piece of land only becomes a building plot if it has planning permission. If you want to build a new home, convert an existing building or add significantly to an existing house, you need planning permission. Building without planning permission or failing to comply with the conditions on a planning permission can lead to drastic action being taken by a district council - new houses built without permission are bulldozed to the ground from time to time. Do not buy a plot unless you are certain of getting planning permission for the house you want to build. This chapter explains the basics of planning permission and tells you the essential points to look for. The right way to make a planning application and what to do if it is refused is fully explained in the companion volume to this book, **How To Get Planning Permission** (see page 3).

Planning permission is given by district councils. The district council has a planning department which deals with planning applications and queries and which keeps planning records. Planning departments employ professional staff called planning or development control officers who assess planning applications, advise planning committees, and decide uncontentious planning applications. Most applications are decided by planning committees made up of councillors who are laypeople elected onto the council. All decisions in Northern Ireland are made by divisional planning officers after consultation with district councillors.

The terms 'planning permission', 'planning approval' and 'planning consent' all have exactly the same meaning. Planning permission relates to the site and not to the person who makes the application. You do not have to own a plot before you make a planning application. If a plot already has planning permission, this does not stop you making another application for a different design or layout. Planning permission does not mean that the owner has to build the house or guarantee that a house can be built, as there can still be legal or practical reasons that prevent it.

There are two kinds of planning permission - outline permission, and detailed or full permission. Detailed permission includes all the details of the proposal - size, style, layout, position within the plot, materials, access, and foul and surface water disposal arrangements. Detailed planning permission is normally given subject to conditions, which sometimes specify further things that have to be approved before construction starts, like a landscaping scheme and samples of building materials.

Outline planning permission establishes the principle that a house can be built on a plot, leaving the design and layout to be settled later. An outline planning permission might specify the type of house and can be subject to a wide range of conditions including the position of the access, and the height or size of the house.

When outline planning permission is given, details of siting, layout, design, access, and landscaping (collectively known as 'reserved matters') can be put forward to the district council in a separate type of application, called a reserved matters application. When both outline planning permission and reserved matters have been approved, the two together are the equivalent of a detailed permission.

FIGURE 11.1   Decision notice granting outline planning permission

COPELAND BOROUGH COUNCIL

Application No.   GR/98/877

TOWN & COUNTRY PLANNING ACT 1990
Applicant: Mr and Mrs K Walford
Agent: FG Miles Consultancy, Western Road, Grinton
Description: OUTLINE APPLICATION - Erection of dwelling and double garage
Address: Land adjoining 'The Larches', Bamborn Road

In pursuance of its powers under the above Act, the council hereby GRANT planning permission for the above development, to be carried out in accordance with the submitted application and plans and subject to compliance with the following conditions:

1 (i) Approval of the details of the siting, design and external appearance of the buildings, the means of access thereto, the treatment of the road surface and the landscaping of the site (hereinafter called the 'reserved matters') shall be obtained from the Local Planning Authority.

   (ii) Application for approval of the reserved matters shall be made to the Local Planning Authority before the expiration of 3 years from the date of this permission.
   Reason: To comply with the requirements of section 91 of the Town & Country Planning Act 1990.

2 The development hereby permitted shall be begun either before the expiration of 5 years from the date of this permission, or before the expiration of 2 years from the date of approval of the last of the reserved matters, whichever is the later.
   Reason: To enable the Local Planning Authority to control the development in detail and to comply with section 91 of the Town and Country Planning Act 1990.

3 At the time of development, and prior to initial occupation of the dwelling, two car parking spaces together with a vehicular turning space, shall be laid out and made available for use in accordance with details to be approved by the Local Planning Authority.
   Reason: In the interests of and for the safety of persons and vehicles using the premises and/or the adjoining road.

4 No development shall take place unless and until there has been submitted to and approved by the Local Planning Authority a scheme of landscaping, which shall include indications of all existing trees and hedgerows on the land, and details of those to be retained, together with measures for their protection in the course of development.
   Reason: In the interests of amenity and of the environment of the development.

5 No development shall be carried out unless and until a schedule of materials and finishes to be used for external walls and roof of the proposed dwelling have been submitted to and approved, in writing, by the Local Planning Authority.
   Reason: To enable the Local Planning Authority to control the development in detail in the interests of amenity by endeavouring to achieve a building of visual quality.

6 No work for the implementation of the development hereby permitted shall be undertaken on the site on public holidays or at any other time except between the hours of 8 a.m. and 6 p.m. on Mondays to Fridays.
   Reason: To safeguard the amenities of nearby residents.

Dated: 10/9/98

Signed:
G. M. Macaulay

DIRECTOR OF PLANNING
For and on behalf of the council

FIGURE 11.2 Location plan

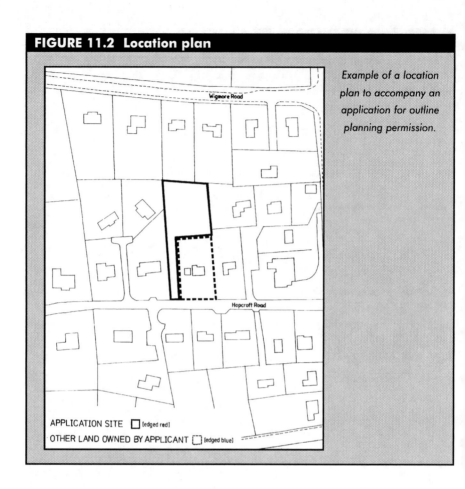

Example of a location plan to accompany an application for outline planning permission.

APPLICATION SITE ☐ [edged red]
OTHER LAND OWNED BY APPLICANT ⬚ [edged blue]

STUDYING THE PLANNING PERMISSION

Study the planning application and permission early on when you assess a plot. The vendors or their agent ought to be able to show you or give you copies, but if not, you can see them or buy copies at the planning department of the district council. You can arrange to have copies sent to you through the post for which there is usually a charge, and you need to give the application reference number.

An outline planning application and permission consists of the application form, a location plan identifying the plot, and the council's decision notice with conditions listed (see Figures 11.1 and 11.2). Any detailed plans submitted with the outline application for illustrative purposes are not strictly speaking part of the permission. Do not rely on them as an indication of what the council will allow you to build. A detailed application and permission includes full site layout plans, floor plans and elevations as well as the

FIGURE 11.3 Decision notice granting detailed planning permission

STRAND DISTRICT COUNCIL

Application No.   CG/98/78

TOWN & COUNTRY PLANNING ACT 1990
Applicant: Mr and Mrs G Knowles
Agent: Jackson Davis Planning Consultants, Western Avenue, Berling
Description: Erection of dwelling
Address: Land adjoining 24 Fir Tree Road, Burnside

In pursuance of its powers under the above Act, the council hereby GRANT planning permission for the above development, in accordance with your application received on 1/2/98 and the plans and particulars accompanying it.

Permission will be subject to the following SIX CONDITIONS:

1 The development hereby permitted shall be begun before the expiration of five years from the date of this permission.
   Reason: To comply with the requirements of section 91 of the Town & Country Planning Act 1990.

2 Prior to the commencement of the development hereby permitted, a schedule and samples of materials and finishes to be used for the external walls and roofs shall be submitted to, and approved in writing by, the local planning authority.
   Reason: To secure a satisfactory external appearance in the interests of amenity.

3 At the time of development, and prior to initial occupation of the dwelling, two car parking spaces together with a vehicular turning space, shall be laid out and made available for use in accordance with the approved plans.
   Reason: In the interests of and for the safety of persons and vehicles using the premises and/or the adjoining road.

4 Before the building hereby permitted is occupied, a close boarded wooden fence 1.8 metres in height shall be erected and thereafter maintained, along the north-eastern boundary of the site.
   Reason: To preserve the privacy and amenity of the adjoining residential property.

5 Before any development takes place, detailed proposals for the planting of trees and/or shrubs for screening the proposed dwelling shall be submitted to and be approved in writing by the District Planning Authority. The approved landscaping scheme shall be implemented not later than the first planting season after occupation of the dwelling or completion of development, whichever is sooner. All failures or plants removed for any reason within five years of planting are to be replaced in the next planting season.
   Reason: To preserve visual amenity and to ensure the creation of a satisfactory environment.

6 All window openings in the south-west and north-east flank walls of the permitted building shall at be glazed with obscured glass only.
   Reason: To preserve the privacy and amenity of the adjoining residential occupiers.

Dated: 8/4/98

Signed:

P. R. Gillan
DIRECTOR OF PLANNING
For and on behalf of the council

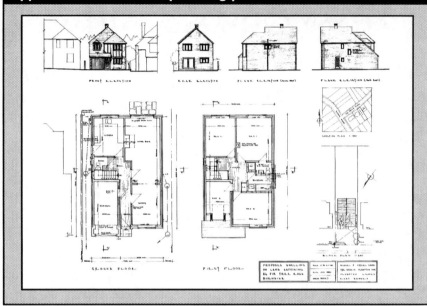

application form, location plan and decision notice (see Figures 11.3 and 11.4). All approved plans and documents should be stamped by the district council. Where plans have been amended or revised, make sure you have the most recent versions.

First check the date of the planning permission. Detailed planning permission expires after five years, unless work is started within that period. Outline planning permission expires after three years, unless an application for approval of reserved matters is made within that time. Work must start within two years of the approval of reserved matters, or within five years from the date of the outline planning permission, whichever is later. If a vendor claims that a planning permission is still valid because work had started, check what was done and ask the district council to confirm in writing that they

agree the works are under way and the planning permission has not expired.

Next look at conditions listed on the decision notice to make sure you are able and willing to meet them, as the council can take action against you if you do not comply with conditions. Typically conditions cover:

◆ Time limits - building work to start within five years.

◆ External materials - samples of building materials to be approved by the district council.

◆ Car parking and turning space - defined areas to be kept clear.

◆ Access - sight lines, construction of kerb and crossover, layout of drive.

◆ Trees, shrubs and hedges - restrictions on felling, protection during construction.

- Landscaping - scheme to be approved by the district council, maintenance of landscaping schemes.
- Drainage - details to be approved by the district council.

Watch particularly for conditions that require other work to be done before the house is built, like an access to be built with clear sight lines or a building to be demolished. Make sure you can get all the necessary rights and consents to fulfil these conditions. There are limits on what councils are supposed to include in conditions but this does not stop them trying it on. One fairly common example you might come across is a limit on the times when the council says building work can take place, such as no work before 9 am or after 6 pm on Monday to Friday, and no working at weekends. This sort of condition should not be placed on a permission unless there are very exceptional circumstances. If you do not fully understand the conditions, speak to your solicitor, a planning officer or a planning consultant.

Study the application plans to check that the boundaries of the application site and of the plot are exactly the same. You might not be able to carry out the planning permission, if you do not own all the land and cannot build according to the plan.

Where you buy a plot with detailed planning permission it is unlikely that you will want to build the house exactly as shown in the permission, so you would need to make a new application for your own design and layout. If your plot has outline planning permission, you can choose between making a reserved matters application or a new detailed application (see page 78). Where your house-type is consistent with the outline permission and you can comply with the conditions, apply for approval of reserved matters. The advantage of this is that the district council only considers the detail of the house, not the principle. When a detailed application is made, the whole question of whether a house should be built on the plot at all can be reviewed.

The safest course is to get planning permission for the house you intend to build before you buy the plot, but since this takes a few months, there is not always time. In this case, find out whether you are likely to get permission. Call in at the planning department and ask to see the file for the existing planning permission. Not all councils are happy to give you their files but the planning application and plans, decision notice and the planning officer's report on the application (see Figure 11.5) are all public documents you are entitled to see.

Find the officer's report in the file; some are an inadequate few lines but others are comprehensive and so very useful to help you assess whether you can get planning permission for what you want. Good reports describe the application, the planning history of the site and local planning policies relevant to the application. If the plot is in or near a Conservation Area, an Area of Outstanding Natural Beauty or National Scenic Area in Scotland, a Site of Special Scientific Interest or has protected trees on it, these facts are noted. The council consults neighbours, the parish council, highway authority and others and their comments are included in the officer's report. The report summarises the planning officer's views and highlights any areas of concern which give you useful pointers for the sort of proposal that will be allowed.

FIGURE 11.5 Planning officer's report to committee

Address: Land adjoining 52 East Drive, Buckleford

Proposal: Outline, Erection of detached house

Application number: An/98/0345

Applicant: Mr and Mrs G Brian

Consultations

Adjoining properties: three letters received, all object, overdevelopment, loss of trees, dangerous access.

Buckleford Conservation Group: object, over development, protected trees at risk.

Borough Engineer: removal of part frontage hedge required to give adequate northerly visibility.

Policies   Borough Plan policies: H2, H3, and ENV7
                 Structure Plan: no conflict
                 Conservation Area: not applicable

Site description

The application site extends to 0.07 hectares of level grassland. It is bounded by established hedgerows and trees on the east and west boundaries and close board fence on the north and south. There is a group of three protected oak trees in the south east corner.

Site History

Previous application for block of six flats refused, 1995

Comment

Housing development is acceptable in principle on this site, which lies within the settlement as defined in the Local Plan. The density of development is slightly higher than that prevailing in the immediate vicinity, but not to such a degree as to cause a loss of amenity. Although only in outline, concern is expressed over the likely proximity of the rear of the house to the protected trees. The submitted site layout plan, whilst not forming part of the application, demonstrates that a dwelling can be accommodated satisfactorily and at an adequate distance from the trees. Formation of the new access requires the loss of part of the frontage hedge to meet the visibility standards of the Borough Engineer. Appropriate landscaping conditions can be attached to the permission requiring the replacement of the hedge. Notwithstanding the local objections, this proposal is considered acceptable.

Recommendation

Grant subject to conditions:
1. Siting, design and materials to be approved
2. Access details to be approved
3. Landscaping, including replacement of part frontage hedge and protection of TPO trees during works
4. Drainage details to be approved

Occasionally you find that the planning officer recommended refusal of the application but that planning permission was nevertheless granted by the committee. This suggests that you might have to deal with a less than enthusiastic planning officer when you put forward your detailed scheme. Ask the planning officer why permission was given.

If the existing planning permission is detailed, look for anything in the report which indicates whether the district council will like or dislike your scheme as opposed to the one approved. For example, the officer could say the scheme was acceptable because the house has a low roof line and the mellow tones of the clay tiles make it relatively unobtrusive. This gives you a clear idea of the sort of design that is likely to be approved.

While you are looking at the planning file of the plot, read any letters from objectors or supporters and from the various consultees. It is of course interesting to know which neighbours objected to an application but, more important, the letters might alert you to possible boundary or other disputes, or to the existence of a restrictive covenant.

PLANNING OFFICER

As well as looking up the file on the existing planning permission, speak to a planning officer about the site and the sort of house you want to build. The officer can usually give you a good idea whether your house would get planning permission or what sort of scheme the council would want to see. What the planning officer says at a meeting, or even in a letter, cannot commit the council when an application is made, so be guided by his comments but do not rely on them totally.

Telephone the planning department, find out which planning officer deals with the area

and make an appointment. Take any plans, drawings or sketches of your house along with you. Ask what constraints might affect the design or site layout and whether he feels that your house type is right for the site. If the officer has objections, discuss them and ask whether they are so significant that planning permission would be turned down. Judging the reaction of a planning officer to a scheme and then deciding what action to take as a result is best done in the light of experience. If in doubt take professional advice.

PROFESSIONAL ADVICE

Whether to get professional help with planning permission depends on your circumstances. If there is a choice of plots in your area of search, it might be easier simply to avoid ones with planning problems. Planning rules and restrictions are very complex, it is better to consult someone who knows the subject, than to get caught out or to just rely on what a planning officer tells you. If you do not have a lot of time to spend on researching the planning situation, use a consultant to do it for you. Where you know that your plans are going to be contentious, get advice to give yourself the maximum chance of success. If you find a piece of land without permission, or without permission for the sort of house you want to build, you can commission a Planning Appraisal Report (see page 157). This will tell you whether you are likely to get permission and how best to go about it. Decide whether your budget can stand the additional professional fees. Spending hundreds of pounds might stop you making a mistake that costs thousands or mean the difference between building your ideal home or not.

Before paying for professional help, you

could get the views of people involved in your project. If you are buying through estate agents, ask what they have to say. Agents who sell plots in the area might know something about local planning policies and what else has been given planning permission. Do not forget that the agent is working for the vendor and has an interest in getting you to buy. Where you are going to buy a house from a selfbuild package company, ask if it has in-house staff who can help. If your problem is straightforward, these people might be able to help but, if it is more complicated, get specialist advice.

If you only want a planning application and drawings prepared, use a building surveyor, architect or architectural technician. If you need advice on getting planning permission, what planning conditions mean, what the planning officer has told you or whether you are likely to get permission for your house, go to a planning consultant. Planning consultants are either chartered surveyors (ARICS or FRICS) or chartered town planners (MRTPI or FRTPI). Surveyors who specialise in planning and development have a broad understanding of the subject, including the relationship between planning and values. Most town planners are trained and work in local government, but some leave to become private consultants. Some people turn to their own local solicitors because of the apparent semi-legal nature of planning but few are specialists in getting planning permission or in dealing with planning practice, policy and procedure.

Apart from the need for planning permission from the district council, there are a number of planning restrictions which can influence what you build on a plot. Where a plot is affected by these, you must look into the implications for your particular scheme.

AGRICULTURAL TIES

Agricultural ties limit the occupancy of a house; they occur in the countryside where planning permission is given for a house specifically for someone working in agriculture. Agriculture includes horticulture and forestry and so covers all manner of farms, small holdings, nurseries and market gardens. A plot with such a restriction can be tied in two ways and one or both might apply. First, planning permission to build a house can include a condition limiting occupation to 'a person solely or mainly working, or last working, in the locality in agriculture or forestry, or a widow or widower of such a person and to any resident dependants'. Second, a building plot can be tied to a farm preventing the plot from being sold, or the occupation of the house restricted, through a legally binding document called a planning obligation, looked at in Chapter 13.

If you build a house on a plot with an agricultural tie and do not come within the definition of who can occupy it, the district council can stop you living there. It is sometimes possible to get round an agricultural occupancy condition, but this is usually where you could get planning permission for a house anyway. You are unlikely to get a condition taken off a plot in the countryside, outside a village. If you cannot satisfy the occupancy restriction or cannot get a new planning permission without an agricultural tie, do not buy the plot. If you

find a sub-standard house with an agricultural tie to demolish and rebuild, it is possible, but not easy, to have the restriction lifted. Again, do not commit yourself to buy until you have planning permission.

ARTICLE 4 DIRECTIONS

Many items of minor building work, which would otherwise need planning permission, are automatically allowed by a government order. This is a practical necessity, preventing district councils being burdened with planning applications for all small alterations and extensions to houses, and for greenhouses, sheds, fences and patios in gardens. These automatic rights (known as 'permitted development') can be taken away by district councils through an Article 4 Direction. You can find out if a plot is affected by an Article 4 Direction from the district council or this may come to light in your solicitors' searches before you buy a plot.

Article 4 Directions are very rare and used mainly in Conservation Areas where district councils want greater control over all types of building. This does not mean you are not allowed, for example, to build a shed in your garden or put up a new fence, rather that you need planning permission to do so. If a plot is in an area covered by an Article 4 Direction, ask a planning officer to explain exactly what is restricted. Do-it-yourself enthusiasts might find having to get planning permission for various projects costly and time consuming.

TREE PRESERVATION ORDERS

District councils can make Tree Preservation Orders (TPOs) on any tree, group of trees or woodland (except fruit trees and orchards) which they think are worth protecting, especially ones that would be affected by new building. In practice councils will put TPOs on literally any tree, how ever small, weak, mis-shapen or common, to give themselves greater control over the development of a site when a planning application is made. This raises the dilemma of whether to cut down unprotected trees that would be in the way, before you make a planning application or even speak to a planning officer.

When full planning permission is granted you can fell TPO trees to make way for the building. A council is less likely to give permission for a scheme which involves losing trees that it has protected, so your plans should aim to minimise effects on TPO trees. Even if you do not mind an oak tree next to your house, the council will still be worried that the next person to live in the house might. District councils will cheerfully make you reduce your plans for a five-bedroom house to a three-bedroom bungalow in the interests of preserving trees which you have no intention of cutting down in any case. Where trees are protected by a TPO (see Figure 12.1), or where a plot is in a Conservation Area, felling or cutting back trees is against the law. If trees could be a problem on a plot, consult a local arboriculturist who can advise you on the merits of particular trees and the scope for felling, cutting back and replacement.

CONSERVATION AREAS

Conservation Areas are designated by district councils to preserve and enhance the architectural or historic interest of an area. The district council can tell you if a plot is in a Conservation Area, and about any special planning policies in the Local Plan which apply to it.

In a Conservation Area planning applications for new houses are closely scrutinised to make sure that the finished building compliments the area. Special attention is paid to design and materials and the district council could insist on the use of local materials (see Figure 12.2) which can add to your costs. Other implications of being in a Conservation Area are:

♦ Trees are automatically protected, as under a TPO.
♦ Demolition of buildings needs Conservation Area consent from the district council.
♦ Greater restrictions on extensions and alterations that can be built without a planning application.
♦ The possibility of an Article 4 Direction requiring planning applications for external alterations, extensions, outbuildings, etc.

If you look at a plot in a Conservation Area, consider whether you would be happy with these constraints. If your plans are for an unusual modern house with facilities in the garden, such as a swimming pool and tennis court, you should perhaps avoid a Conservation Area. However, there are benefits to being in a Conservation Area: they are generally attractive and there is less chance of new building changing the character of the area.

OTHER DESIGNATED AREAS

Other places where there are planning restrictions include Green Belts, National Parks, Areas of Outstanding Natural Beauty or National Scenic Areas, and Sites of Special Scientific Interest. These are shown in Local

FIGURE 12.1 Example Tree Preservation Order (TPO)

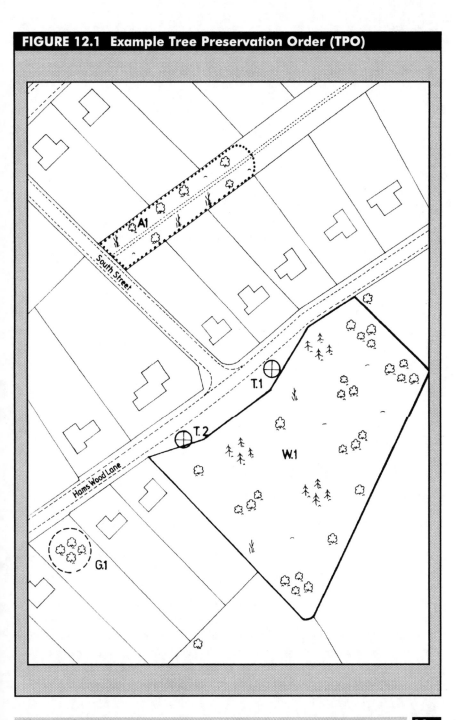

FIGURE 12.1 Example Tree Preservation Order (TPO) Cont...

SCHEDULE

No. on map	Description	Situation

*Trees specified individually
(encircled in black on the map)*

| T.1 | 1 Oak | Land adj Hams Wood Lane Branchley |
| T.2 | 1 Ash | As above |

*Trees specified by reference to an Area
(within a dotted black line on the map)*

| A.1 | Area consisting of scattered specimens of Ash, Oak, Birch | Land adj South Street |

*Groups of trees
(within a broken black line on the map)*

| G.1 | 6 Oaks | Land adj Hams Wood Lane, Branchley |

*Woodlands
(within a continuous black line on the map)*

| W.1 | Mixed deciduous woodland comprising: Oak,Ash, Birch, Pine | As above |

Plans, which also contain particular planning policies that apply to them.

Green Belts are formally designated areas of land around cities, where strict planning policies aim to prevent all but a few limited types of development. The term 'Green Belt' is frequently misused and does not mean any open land around all towns and cities. Since planning permission is harder to get in a Green Belt, check the existing permission very carefully. If you hope to demolish and replace an existing building, look up the relevant Local Plan policies as there could be size restrictions on replacements.

National Parks have their own authorities which deal with planning, drawing up Local Plans and deciding planning applications in the park. In National Parks there are fewer 'permitted development' rights to carry out minor building works. If you plan to build in a

FIGURE 12.2 New house in a Conservation Area

The design and materials of new houses in Conservation Areas are carefully controlled by councils' planning departments, like the use of flint walls on this house to match existing flint walls in the area. This can affect the size and style of the house and building costs, and needs to be taken into account in assessing and valuing a plot.

National Park, and extend the house later, check carefully whether you would get permission.

Areas of Outstanding Natural Beauty (AONBs) and National Scenic Areas (NSAs) in Scotland, are designated to preserve the landscape. 'Permitted development' rights are restricted, the design and materials of new buildings are supposed to reflect local architecture, and new buildings have to be sited unobtrusively.

Sites of Special Scientific Interest (SSSIs) protect wildlife and geological features. If your plot is near an SSSI, speak to a planning officer and look in the Local Plan to find out what restrictions apply.

CHAPTER 13 LEGAL CONSIDERATIONS

PLANNING OBLIGATIONS

In order to get planning permission, owners sometimes sign a legal document called a planning obligation, also termed a 'planning agreement' or 'section 106 agreement', or 'section 50 agreement' in Scotland. This can restrict how land is used, limit what building takes place, or make an applicant bear the cost of off-site works needed before building can go ahead. For example, planning obligations could prevent domestic buildings being built on part of the site, provide for a contribution towards the cost of a new drainage scheme or require part of the plot to be given to the district council for a public footpath.

Planning obligations are legal charges on the land and so if you buy a plot subject to a planning obligation, you are bound by its terms. The vendor should tell you about a planning obligation; in any case it will be in the planning records and noted by your solicitor in his standard pre-purchase searches.

Planning obligations can be enforced by district councils and are not easy to remove. This has to be done by agreement with the council or, with modern ones, after five years you can apply to the council to remove it, with a right of appeal if this is refused. You must show that removal would not harm the area, that the restriction or requirement is obsolete or that a reasonable use of the land is being prevented.

You might come across similar legal agreements, made under the Highways Acts, which require works to a road or access, or a contribution to road improvements, before building takes place. Planning obligations and highway agreements usually affect the value of a plot which should be taken into account

before you make an offer. You must find out precisely what your obligations would be and have any questions settled by your solicitor.

COVENANTS

A covenant is a binding private agreement between individuals. In Scotland, agreements similar to covenants are known as ancient feus. When buying a plot, purchasers often agree covenants with vendors, for example, to build fences, improve drives, or get vendors' approval of detailed house plans. More important are restrictive covenants that control the way in which a plot is used or developed. They are legally binding and are designed to prevent something from happening on one piece of land, that would otherwise disadvantage another. This is why they occur where a larger area of land is sub-divided. For example, a large estate might sell off land with restrictive covenants prohibiting houses being built or limiting the height of any houses, to preserve views from the main house. Another common situation where covenants are imposed is when house owners sell off part of their garden as a plot. To protect the existing house, the owner might state that there can be no commercial use of the new house, specify any trees that must be retained or say that no first-floor windows should overlook the garden of the original house. For examples of what covenants involve, see Figures 13.1, 13.2, and 13.3.

Planning permission does not override restrictive covenants, so even if you get permission to build a two-storey house, a covenant limiting building to single-storey can stop you from carrying out the planning permission. Old restrictive covenants that no longer seem to serve a useful purpose can be troublesome because it might not be clear whether they would be enforced. For example, a plot could have a covenant dating from 1910 restricting building, but meanwhile a housing estate, supermarket and bypass have separated the plot from the property with the benefit of the covenant. It is difficult to imagine why anybody connected with the original property would be concerned about a building on the plot now, yet a remote possibility remains that the breach of covenant would be noticed. To guard against this, you can take out insurance to cover any claim that might be made. This can be arranged by your solicitor who should advise you on anything to do with covenants.

You can have restrictive covenants removed or relaxed by agreement with the person who has the benefit of the covenant. You are likely to have to pay for this and if the covenant means the difference between building or not, the price will probably be a large proportion of the plot's potential value.

FIGURE 13.1 Examples of covenants

Erecting a fence:

Save to the extent that the property is already fenced the Purchaser hereby covenants to erect and maintain a good and sufficient fence along the boundaries edged in red of a height and style first approved in writing by the Vendor.

Single dwelling only:

For the benefit and protection of such part or parts of the land edged in blue on the plan bound up within as are vested in the Vendor at the date of this deed and so as to bind the property into whosoever hands the same may come the Purchaser for himself and his successors in title hereby covenants with the vendor not to erect upon the property any building other than one private dwelling house with appropriate outbuildings and not to use the same except for occupation as a single private residence.

EASEMENTS, WAYLEAVES AND PRIVATE RIGHTS OF WAY

Easements are rights over land such as private rights of way, and rights to maintain pipes and cables. When inspecting a plot, look out for well-trodden footpaths, manhole covers, and cables or pylons as these could point to the existence of easements.

Easements for sewers and water mains usually cover a strip of land above and on either side of the pipe. The water company has the right of access to that land for maintenance and also to dig up and replace the pipe, but they would have to reinstate your garden. If your plot has pipes or cables running through it, contact the service company concerned to find out the size, depth and age of the pipe and the likelihood of any works being carried out. Ask how any new pipe would be laid, as microtunnelling techniques now avoid the need to dig huge trenches.

Wayleaves are similar to easements and usually the term is used in connection with electricity supply cables where the supply company has a wayleave to carry cables over or under a plot. If pylons or other apparatus are involved, a small annual payment could be made by the supply company for 'rent' of the land involved.

FIGURE 13.2 Examples of Covenants on a Plot

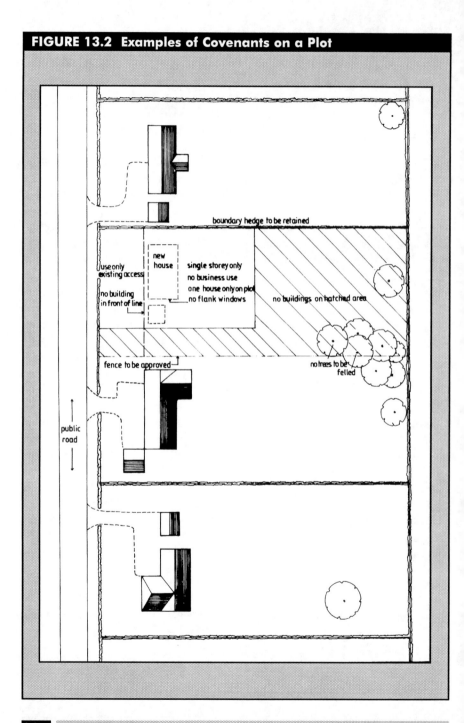

boundary hedge to be retained

new
house

single storey only
no business use
one house only on plot
no flank windows

use only
existing access

no building
in front of line

no buildings on hatched area

fence to be approved

no trees to be
felled

public
road

Legal Considerations

Sometimes there are private rights of way over a plot, either for pedestrians only, or for vehicles as well. These can be diverted or removed by agreement, but removal is unlikely if the right of way is the only access to someone else's land. It is possible for rights of way to become established where they have been used unimpeded, over a long period of time, usually at least 20 years. Look for gates and tracks on the plot and, if somebody claims to have walked across it for the last 30 years and has every intention of continuing to do so, do not dismiss the claim out of hand.

Some plots have the benefit of rights over other land. This might simply be a right of access over a private road. Ancient rights over common land still exist in many areas, such as Verderers' rights in the New Forest, and Commoners' rights on Ashdown Forest. Coastal plots can have rights of access to the foreshore. These rights do not usually have cost implications for the owner, and are more likely to be selling points for the property. Of course, if you do happen to own a herd of swine, you might find a right to fatten them on acorns from the local wood of some benefit.

FOOTPATHS AND BRIDLEWAYS

Public footpaths and bridleways are usually evident on the ground, may be signposted and are marked on Ordnance Survey maps. Highway authorities keep definitive maps of public rights of way which you should inspect if there are any doubts about the existence or route of a path. If a path would hamper building on a plot, you can apply to have it diverted but not until you own the plot. If you want to divert a footpath before buying, the vendor has to apply either on his behalf or on

FIGURE 13.3 Site with legal restrictions

Your solicitor must research ownership and legal restrictions thoroughly before you buy a plot. Covenants or ransom strips can prevent building on apparently obvious plots, like this undeveloped site in a country town.

yours. Applications are to the county or district council for a public path diversion order and you will probably have to pay the council's costs. If the diversion order is opposed, it must be confirmed by the appropriate Secretary of State and compensation is payable to anyone whose rights are harmed by diversion. Discuss the procedure and cost with the district council before applying.

Public rights of way are not extinguished by the grant of planning permission. So, if you get planning permission to build a house across a footpath, you still need to get a public path diversion order before building works start. The council will have considered the effect on the path as part of their normal planning application assessment. Anyone likely to object to diversion of the footpath would probably have objected to the planning application. Finding likely objectors is useful as you might be able to persuade them not to object to the diversion order.

ASSESSING YOUR PLOT - CHECK LIST

Use this check list as a basis for your assessment of a plot. These factors can affect value, restrict what you build, or stop you building. Do not commit yourself to buying a plot until you have checked each point on the list.

◆ **First Considerations**
   Adequate size for house type
   Lie of the land
   Ground conditions
   Trees
   Obstacles
   Orientation
   Boundaries
   Adjoining uses

◆ **Access**
   Type of road (public/private)
   Rights to use private road
   Rights of access over other
      land/ransom strip
   Highway authority standards
   Sight lines at access point
   Parking and turning space

◆ **Services**
   Method of foul drainage
      (public/private system)
   Method of surface water drainage
      (public/soakaway/watercourse)
   Rights of access to drains

   Water supply
   Electricity, gas, telephone
   Costs of connection

◆ **Planning permission**
   Type of permission (outline/detailed)
   Date of permission
   Conditions
   Application plans
   Planning officer's report
   Contact the planning officer

◆ **Planning restrictions**
   Agricultural ties
   Article 4 Directions
   Tree Preservation Orders (TPO)
   Conservation Area
   Other designated areas

◆ **Legal considerations**
   Planning obligations
   Restrictive covenants
   Easements, wayleaves and private
      rights of way
   Footpaths and bridleways

PART 4 VALUING YOUR PLOT

You have found a building plot to buy, it is in the right place and suitable for the house you want to build - but what about the price? Is the asking price reasonable? Is it in line with other plots? How much should you pay? What should you offer?

These are the key questions which you face and you must find answers to them - if you do not want to pay too much or risk losing the plot. You need to know what factors affect values, how to value land and how to work out where to pitch your offer. This Part gives you that information and takes you through the valuation process to making an offer.

The value of a plot is influenced by a wide range of factors, from the state of the economy through to the nature of the underlying soil. National and local property markets set a general level for plot prices in an area. The value of an individual plot is then determined by what can be built on the site and the cost of the build. We look first at the wider influence on plot values: market conditions.

Plot values are directly related to the housing market - national, regional and local. At the national level, following a large fall at the end of the 1980s and in the early 1990s, land prices rose gradually then sharply, closely following the fortunes of the housing market. National trends can be misleading, however, as they do not reflect wide regional variations. These are important if you think of relocating. Find out whether prices are falling or rising in each region, as what is happening in your area, or nationally, might not be happening elsewhere. For example, during the early 1990s, building land values fell by 17 per cent in outer London, rose by 4 per cent in Northern Ireland and remained static in Scotland.

As well as differing between regions, prices also vary significantly within each region. Generalisations like, 'property prices in the south-east are the highest in the country' can be misleading. Whilst this might be true of somewhere like Guildford in Surrey, it is certainly not true of, say, Southampton in Hampshire or Gillingham in Kent, where prices are well below the national average.

Many local factors influence plot prices, including:

◆ Proximity to motorways and main line stations.

◆ Distance to towns and cities.
◆ Local employment prospects.
◆ Character of the surrounding countryside.
◆ Character of the locality.
◆ Availability of building plots.
◆ Councils' planning policies.

These affect demand and supply and so establish price levels. Most people want to live in places with access to well-paid jobs, schools, leisure and shopping facilities, and in pleasant surroundings. Others are attracted to unspoilt countryside or villages and towns of particular character. Where continuing demand coincides with limited opportunities to build new houses, plot prices will be relatively high.

Prices can fluctuate across a county with values higher close to towns and main transport links and lower in the areas in between. There can be spots of higher values where the landscape or scenery is exceptional, or in sought after, picturesque towns and villages. Even within a town or village, there could be an expensive part - perhaps a Conservation Area around the church or green; and a cheaper part - near a factory or railway siding.

Within a local property market, the main factor which fixes a plot's value is the level of prices paid for similar plots in the vicinity. Sales provide a reference point to establish value and to judge the level of demand. When a plot sells after a number of offers have been made for it, a comparable plot in the area is likely to attract equal interest and the same sort of price. Remember, the real test is what plots actually sell for, not their asking prices.

FIGURE 14.1 Existing house prices determine plot values

The value of a building plot is directly related to the value of house that can be built on it. Finding out local house prices in order to value these two plots is straightforward because of the number of similar new houses close by.

All the factors looked at so far determine, generally, the value of a plot. To establish the value of a particular plot, you need to know:

◆ Exactly what can be built on the plot.
◆ What it would cost to build.
◆ The market value of the finished house.

The answer to the first question is governed by all the points covered in Part Three: physical features, access, services, planning permission, planning restrictions and legal considerations. All except private legal matters are taken into account when a planning application is made and so it is the planning permission that primarily dictates what can be built. This affects value directly - a 0.25 acre plot with permission for a house of 120 sq m (1,200 sq ft) worth £25,000 could be worth £50,000 with permission for a 300 sq m (3,000 sq ft) house.

When you value a plot look carefully at the planning permission, but also consider its potential for a larger house, or for more houses, than currently permitted.

The second key question, the cost of the build, depends mainly on the size and type of dwelling, and the materials and finishes. You also need to take account of unusual costs associated with a particular site, because of its ground conditions, physical restrictions, or legal constraints, for example.

You need to answer the third question in order to value a plot, even if you have no intention of selling. The market value of any land is derived from the value of what can be built on it. So the market value of a plot is derived from what the finished house would fetch. The price level of similar houses in the area shows what your house would be worth (see Figure 14.1).

Factors Determining Value

CHAPTER 15 VALUATION METHODS

Valuation is not a precise science; it is a means of estimating what price a plot would fetch in the market. The simplest form of valuation, and usually the most reliable, is a comparison with other sales. The more sales evidence you have, the better picture you build up of the local plot market, and the more accurate your figure. For example: if five plots each with permission for a four-bedroom detached house have sold recently in the same area for £50,000, £48,000, £51,500, £49,500 and £50,500, then you know that the value of a similar plot will be around £50,000. In practice you do not usually find so many consistent sales so you have to make a comparison between the plot you are valuing and ones that have sold. This is illustrated in the comparable sales table (see Figure 15.1). Compare plots in terms of planning permission, size of plot, type of area, setting, and physical features. Use house prices to help gauge differences in values between areas. Having made your comparison with other plot sales, remember to deduct any unusual building costs that were not reflected in the prices paid for other plots.

A simple rule-of-thumb method of valuing building plots is used by developers and agents to get an initial idea of value and to see whether an asking price looks reasonable (see Figure 15.2). This involves looking at plot prices as a percentage of the value of the completed house, or its 'resale' value as it is sometimes called. So where a plot sells for £25,000 and the finished house would sell for £100,000, the percentage paid is 25 per cent.

Your contacts among estate agents involved in plot sales, can give you an idea of the sort of percentages being paid and the approximate value of the house you want to build. For example: if you want to build a three-bedroom chalet bungalow and these are currently selling at around £75,000, and the percentage being paid locally for plots is about 33 per cent, the plot value is going to be around 33 per cent of £75,000, that is, £25,000.

There is no set percentage as it varies according to the state of the market and the nature and scarcity of the plot concerned, but typically the figure is between 25 per cent and 35 per cent. During housing booms percentages of 50 per cent or even more can be paid, but the level can slump to below 25 per cent in a depressed housing market. In a rising market, developers assume high sales figures in their calculations to reflect likely price rises during the time it takes to build the house. In a falling market, the opposite is true and developers are pessimistic about the prices they will get. Unless you believe values will rise or fall significantly in the near future, use current house prices.

Do not rely on rule-of-thumb alone unless you can get good local information on the right percentage to use, based on a reasonable volume of recent sales.

The comparable and rule-of-thumb methods of valuation tell you the market value of a plot. There is another method which tells you how much a site is worth, based on your particular scheme - a residual valuation. This is a mathematical calculation of value, starting with an estimate of what the finished house would be worth, then deducting all your build, finance and other costs, to arrive at a residual value for the plot. You can also use the method in reverse to find out if a plot price is reasonable. Take the asking price of the plot, add on the build costs, and see if the total compares with prices of similar houses. An example residual valuation is shown in Figure 15.3.

FIGURE 15.1 Valuing a plot using comparable sales

Plot to be valued:

0.20 acres with planning permission for 4 bed chalet in an established residential area

Comparables:

Plot	Analysis	Sale price (£)
Fox's Lane, Brington	Similar plot, but larger and better position not on an estate	50,000
Collins Walk Brington	Good comparable, in a residential area but slightly larger	45,000
Hall Barn Road Wedling	Planning permission only for 3 bed chalet, next to petrol station	35,000
Harris Road Brington	On country lane, has views, much larger, next to open countryside	65,000
Fox's lane Brington	Adjoins woodland, established garden, has existing access drive	47,500

Conclusion:	Collins Walk plot is most similar to the plot being valued but is slightly larger and this should be reflected by deducting £500 in the valuation. The other plots with higher sale prices were larger or in better positions. The plot with a lower price had disadvantages. **The value of the plot is therefore £44,500.**

Developers use residual valuations to calculate the maximum amount that they can afford to spend on plots. Their figures have to include full labour costs, profit and overheads. If you are doing some or all of the work yourself or do not need to make a profit, it is up to you whether to include these as costs in your valuation. If you do not, you will have a higher plot value.

The residual method is useful where your build involves unusual costs or where there are not enough recent sales on which to base a comparable valuation, but it can produce misleading answers if incorrect data are used.

Valuation Methods

FIGURE 15.2 Valuing a plot using the rule-of-thumb method

Sales of other plots:

Plot	Estimated value of house (£)	Sale price of plot (£)	% plot price of house value
Fox's Lane, Brington	151,000	50,000	33%
Collins Walk, Brington	128,500	45,000	35%
Hall Barn Road, Wedling	125,000	35,000	28%
Harris Road, Brington	191,000	65,000	34%
Fox's Lane, Brington	135,500	47,500	35%

Average percentage paid for plot =   **33%**

Estimated value of finished house on plot to be valued	@ rule-of-thumb %	=	value of plot
£135,000	**@ 33%**	**=**	**£44,500**

An agent tells you that plots are fetching 'about 33 per cent of resale'. He estimates that a house of the type that you want to build will be worth around £135,000 (the 'resale' value), which means that the plot will be worth 33 per cent of £135,000, or £44,500. To check the correct percentage to apply, look at plot and new house prices locally. Try to find properties that are as closely comparable to yours as possible and make a table of them, as here, to calculate the average percentage paid per plot.

In one case a valuer engaged by a bank produced a detailed residual valuation showing that a plot was worth less than nothing, although the same plot sold a month later for £75,000. Residual valuations are also helpful because they necessitate a detailed examination of the costs and show any potential profit in a scheme. Computer enthusiasts can set up a residual valuation on a spreadsheet and run it making different assumptions about the figures, for example the value of the completed house, or the effect of an additional £5,000 of unforeseen expenses. Although many developers use computer programs to produce residual valuations, do use the results with caution and do not lose sight of what the market tells you a plot is worth.

FIGURE 15.3 Valuing a plot using the residual method

Value of house

Anticipated value of finished house		135,000
Less agents and legal fees if sold @ 2.5%		<u>3,375</u>
Net proceeds of sale		131,625

Building costs

Build costs, £37 sq ft x 1,500 sq ft	55,500	
Garage	7,500	
Access and services	<u>4,000</u>	
Subtotal	67,000	
Contingency, say 10%	6,700	
Professional fees, say 2%	<u>1,300</u>	
Build cost	75,000	
Finance on build, 11% over 6 months	4,125	
Profit @ 10%	<u>7,500</u>	
Total building costs		<u>86,625</u>
Balance available for purchasing plot		45,000
Less legal fees on plot purchase, say		<u>650</u>
Balance available to buy land		44,350
Value of plot		**£44,500**

This valuation assumes a high level of contingency costs, and a profit level of 10 per cent. The resulting figure available for the plot purchase is therefore conservative, being the level that a developer would be likely to pay. A selfbuilder could eliminate the profit, and the costs of selling the completed house, to arrive at a higher figure.

By the time you have studied agents' particulars and viewed some plots, you will start to have a feel for values and for what you can get for your money. If you want to check the value more precisely, and make sure that you are paying the right sort of price, carry out your own valuation. In practice, it is best to use all three basic methods of valuation described in the last chapter and compare the figures.

First, try to get as much information as possible on plot sales and prices of houses similar to the one you want to build. This provides the raw data to feed into your valuations. Find actual sale prices rather than asking prices. While you are searching for plots, ask estate agents about plots they have sold in the area, how much they sold for and what percentage of the finished house price this represented. Find out at the same time who is buying plots - individuals or builders/developers - as this could influence the offer you make later. Agents are reluctant to give precise figures on sales, especially where sales have not yet been completed. They might say whether the asking price was exceeded or whether the price went over, say, £50,000, which would give you an idea of the price paid. Auction results give a good indication of market value and, because they are held in public, the agent is more likely to tell you the result. Keep a note of anything you learn, to use in your calculations - the more local and recent the information, the more accurate your valuation will be.

Find out house prices from estate agents' advertisements in local newspapers and in estate agents' windows. Where you buy a plot through agents, ask them to put a figure on the house you intend to build. Tell them precisely the size and style of house and show them any drawings, so they can then give you a more specific price. If you are on good terms with other estate agents, try asking them for a figure as well.

Once you have done your market research, carry out your valuations. Where you can find out about recent sales of similar plots, market value is best gauged by comparing your plot with those sales. Do this exactly as described in the previous chapter. Note the location and appearance of the other plots in order to make a proper comparison with yours. Making adjustments to reflect any differences between plots is not scientific, but depends on sensible judgements. Details of one sale of a near identical plot are a better basis for valuation than of any number where there are significant differences. Use all the available information to reach a figure.

A rule-of-thumb percentage valuation is very straightforward, where there is a good indication of what percentage of house prices is being paid for plots. Apply this to the value of your house when finished, to arrive at a figure for the plot.

A residual valuation takes time to carry out but it is worthwhile because it gives you a land price based on your own project and shows whether your project is financially sound. The budget prepared before you started looking for a plot shows the maximum amount of money available to buy it. You can use much of the information in your budget to do a residual valuation. Get more detailed figures on building costs and finance, if you need them, from your selfbuild package company or building designer and from your bank or building society.

Use the example residual valuation given in the last chapter as a guide (see Figure

15.3). Decide whether you want to include profit and full labour and finance costs in your calculation. Builders and developers have to include these costs, but other individuals do not and this can be reflected in the amount they are prepared to offer for a plot.

Valuing a plot is more complicated where development potential is involved. A plot with planning permission for a modest house might be able to take a much larger house; there might be planning permission for one house, but enough space for two. The extent to which any potential should be reflected in the price you pay depends on the likelihood of getting planning permission. To value potential, work out what the plot would be worth if an improved planning permission was given and compare that figure with what the plot is worth with its existing permission. The difference between these is the maximum additional value that could possibly be realised and a proportion of this can be reflected in the price. The right proportion depends on the chances of getting planning permission and is usually anything up to about two thirds. So, if the current value of a plot is £30,000, but with a new permission would be £50,000, and the prospects for a new permission are good, you might decide the potential is worth £7,000 (50,000 - 30,000 = 20,000 x say 35% = £7,000). Unless there is a realistic prospect of getting planning permission, ignore development potential in your figures. Vendors naturally tend to overstate potential and the only way to put this beyond doubt is to make a planning application but, if permission is given, the vendor would probably want to be paid the full value.

Where potential is involved, or where the valuation of a plot is complex, consider taking professional advice, ideally from a locally-based firm of chartered surveyors or valuers which is involved in the building plot market. Advice can vary from an opinion of value through to a formal report and valuation. If you have done some of the ground-work yourself, for example, finding out about comparable sales, give the information to the valuer as it might save him time and you money. In a complex case you might pay several hundred pounds for a formal valuation, but if this saves you several thousand pounds it is money well spent.

So far we have looked at how to calculate the market value of a plot objectively. Remember that, in doing a valuation, you are making an estimate of what a site will fetch. No matter what sum your calculations produce, a piece of land is ultimately worth what someone is prepared to pay for it. There are other factors which you might need to take into account when it actually comes to making an offer.

Each plot you look at inevitably has an element of value personal to you, reflecting your own preferences and circumstances. You might attach personal value to: locations near family, workplace, or existing house; a view; established gardens; being close to open countryside; or being able to buy quickly or at a certain time. None of these things can be valued objectively; it is for you to judge how much they are worth.

Although you should not lay too much weight on the vendor's asking price, it is still a factor which you need to take into account in working out what offer to make. If no asking price is quoted, ask the selling agent what he thinks the vendor would accept. Asking prices are usually not too far from the market value, but there are always exceptions. Some

Your Valuation and Offer

vendors try it on by asking unreasonably high figures, but this should not stop you making a lower offer. In a rising market asking prices are often exceeded by prices actually paid, and in a falling market vendors often have to take less than the asking price. In Scotland, asking prices are set low and offers are invited above the figure given.

Sometimes a plot is put on the market at what appears to be well below market value. You might have stumbled upon a vendor who is desperate, wants a very quick sale, or has been badly advised. More likely, the low price reflects a problem like a covenant, a ransom strip, an inconvenient right of way across the land, or unstable ground conditions. Ask the vendor or his agent whether the site has any problems and, if nothing is apparent on the ground, warn your solicitor of this if a sale goes ahead.

In talking to the vendor or his agent try to find out whether other people are interested in the plot and whether they are likely to make offers. If you are the only person interested in a particular plot, you might be able to buy it for far less than its theoretical value. On the other hand, another keen purchaser might be willing to pay well over the general market value. You need to reflect the level and strength of competition in your figure.

Before you put forward an offer you should have formed a view on the market value, calculated what you can afford to pay and decided what the plot is worth to you. You should also have an idea of the vendor's expectations - either a price, or at least an indication of the sort of figure that would be accepted. The right level for your offer depends on the state of the market, the likelihood of other competing bids, and how much you want that particular plot. Professional advice can help you to an extent, but ultimately the decision on how much to pay for a plot rests with you.

VALUING YOUR PLOT - CHECK LIST

◆ Find out the asking price.

◆ Look for information on comparable plot sales.

◆ Find out the level of house prices and estimate what your finished house will be worth.

◆ Carry out comparable, rule-of-thumb and residual valuations.

◆ Consider whether to get a professional valuation.

◆ Decide on how much to offer based on your valuations and taking account of personal factors, the market and competition, and the vendor's expectations.

PART 5 BUYING YOUR PLOT

Plots are sold in different ways and each method has its opportunities and pitfalls. There are tactics which you can use in putting forward offers and negotiating, to secure your purchase successfully. Competition for plots can be fierce and, unless you know what goes on behind the scenes, you could well be unsuccessful. This Part guides you through the steps involved in buying your plot and highlights the action that you should take.

CHAPTER 17 BUYING LAND

Most building plots are sold by private treaty, exactly as houses are bought and sold. In this chapter we look at the main parties involved in a purchase, and follow the private treaty procedure through to completing a purchase.

KEY PLAYERS

The key players in the purchase of a building plot are:

◆ The vendor
◆ The vendor's agent
◆ You, the purchaser
◆ The two parties' solicitors or licensed conveyancers
◆ Any competing buyers

Vendors may be private individuals, companies, local authorities, trusts, organisations, in fact almost anybody. Most plots are sold by private individuals, builders and developers and, in some areas, by local authorities. Their willingness to negotiate, supply information, act quickly, and co-operate generally varies, although most recognise that it is in their interests to help you as much as possible.

Vendors' agents differ enormously in their approach to the task of selling a plot. Some remain behind their desks, and do nothing to help, saying that it is for you to satisfy yourself about planning, drainage, services and all other points. Others will be found crashing about in the brambles, banging in site boundary markers, peering into drains and measuring sight lines at the access. They might give you copies of planning documents, letters from service companies and details of the size and depth of the nearest sewer. Whichever camp the agents fall in, make sure they recognise that you are a serious buyer.

Do not forget that they are not working for you, but for the vendor. However, if helping you speeds the arrival of their commission cheque, you can expect some degree of service from them. Do not hesitate to ask agents questions, but always check the answers for yourself. This applies especially to anything that could affect the cost or your ability to build the house you want on the plot.

Anybody can be an estate agent and sell building plots, regardless of qualifications. Those with professional training will be members of the Royal Institution of Chartered Surveyors (RICS), Incorporated Society of Valuers and Auctioneers (ISVA) or the National Association of Estate Agents (NAEA). You can expect a professional approach from members of these organisations, but membership does not guarantee knowledge or experience of selling development land. If an agent, qualified or not, seems to have no idea what he is talking about, try talking directly to the vendor.

Solicitors and conveyancers too have different levels of knowledge and experience with building plots. Most deal with buying and selling plots from their desks, a practical necessity if they are based 200 miles from the site. Stay in touch with your solicitor throughout your purchase, but do not try to contact the vendor's solicitor. He is unlikely to speak to you, as solicitors do not like short-circuiting long-winded lines of communication.

Competing buyers are always a threat to your purchase, right up to exchange of contracts. Some could be professional developers with knowledge of planning, much experience of buying plots and armed with computers to check their valuations. They also hold an ace card with which to woo the estate

FIGURE 17.1 Plot for sale

When you see a plot for sale be ready to move quickly. Contact the estate agents to let them know you are interested and stay in touch with them throughout the purchase.

agent - the finished house to sell - earning the agent a second commission from the same piece of land. Do not be put off. Developers, builders, speculators and investors have to make a profit after staff have been paid and the finished house marketed, advertised and sold. This gives you an ace card too - the ability to outbid the developer.

Other people might be after the same plot. If you are better prepared and ready to move quickly, you can snap it up before they have put together their offer. Detailed and accurate budgeting could give you the confidence to offer that extra £500 needed to secure the plot, without risking your scheme's viability.

PRIVATE TREATY SALES

In England, Wales and Northern Ireland most plots are sold by private treaty. In Scotland some sales are conducted by private treaty, but the majority take place through a different system, where sealed bids are submitted and the deal becomes binding on acceptance of a bid. As this is a type of tender, the system in Scotland is examined in Chapter 20.

There are three distinct stages in a purchase by private treaty:

◆ Negotiations prior to an offer being accepted.
◆ Accepting an offer to exchange of contracts.

◆ Exchange of contracts to completion of the purchase.

The chart in Figure 17.2 shows the private treaty procedure, explaining what buyers and their solicitors do at the different stages of a transaction. Procedure varies slightly depending on whether the title of the plot is registered. There is nothing terribly complicated about private treaty sales procedure, although legal documents are not always easy to understand, being littered with obscure language and entirely lacking in any form of punctuation. It is technically possible for you to do your own conveyancing, but this is not a good idea for a plot purchase. If you build your own home, you will be saving money, so invest a small part of this in a good solicitor or licensed conveyancer - it is money well spent.

The first stage of the purchase is negotiation, which comprises everything that happens before an offer is accepted by the vendor. During this time you may make all the right moves, but you have no control over the outcome. It is only when your offer is accepted by the vendor that you start to move towards a formal agreement to buy. Negotiations are usually carried out 'subject to contract'. This means that nothing agreed is legally binding until contracts are exchanged, preventing you being caught out, if a problem with the plot comes to light, after an offer has been accepted but before exchange of contracts. Letters concerning sales are often marked 'subject to contract', although this is not necessary.

When your offer is accepted, the vendor's agent usually draws up a memorandum of sale. This is not a legal document and merely says what has been agreed, the names of the vendor and purchaser and their solicitors. It could be a formal-looking document, as in the example (see Figure 17.3), or simply a letter. It is normally sent to all the people listed on it, together with a copy of the sales particulars. If there is no agent involved, inform your solicitors and give them the name of the vendor's solicitor. Offer and acceptance should be confirmed in writing to avoid misunderstandings.

Once your offer has been accepted the solicitors or conveyancers will set to work. Before exchange of contracts your solicitor carries out searches and sends enquiries about the property to the vendor's solicitor. The searches involve inspecting the local land charges register, and sending a list of standard questions to the district council. Any covenants or easements should come to light at this stage, plus information on any major development or road schemes that affect the site. Information you get about proposed or likely development is very limited in standard searches and so consider commissioning a Planning Search (see page 159). In addition to the solicitor's normal searches, and before contracts are exchanged, you should check:

◆ That planning permission will be given for exactly what you want to build.
◆ That all service and drainage connections can be made (and the costs involved).
◆ If ground conditions are poor, the cost of special foundations.
◆ That the precise boundaries of the site are clear.
◆ That finance arrangements are agreed and the bank or building society's solicitor is instructed to deal with any new mortgage.

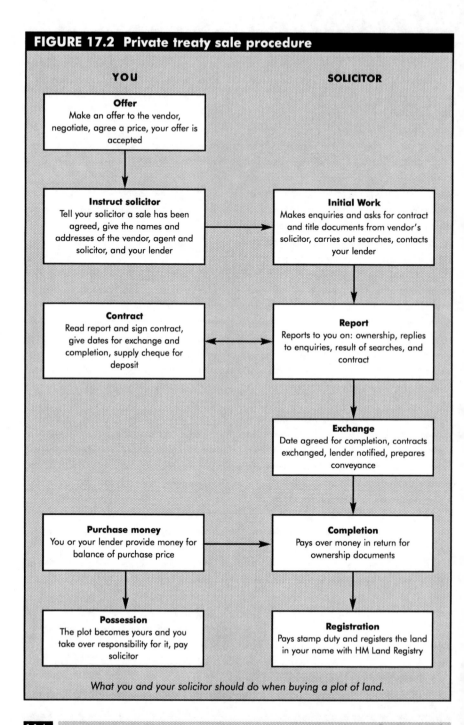

FIGURE 17.2 Private treaty sale procedure

YOU

SOLICITOR

Offer
Make an offer to the vendor, negotiate, agree a price, your offer is accepted

Instruct solicitor
Tell your solicitor a sale has been agreed, give the names and addresses of the vendor, agent and solicitor, and your lender

Initial Work
Makes enquiries and asks for contract and title documents from vendor's solicitor, carries out searches, contacts your lender

Contract
Read report and sign contract, give dates for exchange and completion, supply cheque for deposit

Report
Reports to you on: ownership, replies to enquiries, result of searches, and contract

Exchange
Date agreed for completion, contracts exchanged, lender notified, prepares conveyance

Purchase money
You or your lender provide money for balance of purchase price

Completion
Pays over money in return for ownership documents

Possession
The plot becomes yours and you take over responsibility for it, pay solicitor

Registration
Pays stamp duty and registers the land in your name with HM Land Registry

What you and your solicitor should do when buying a plot of land.

Remember that once contracts are exchanged, you cannot pull out of your purchase without paying a penalty.

Make certain that the sale plans, the site boundaries, and what you believe you are buying, are all one and the same. Boundary disputes often occur when land is sold, either between vendor and purchaser or between a new owner and neighbours. To avoid disputes, get a plan showing measured boundaries that are pegged out on site and agreed by all parties. The best way to do this is to meet the vendor or his agent on site, agree and mark out boundaries with wooden posts banged well in, and then take measurements. This is particularly important where, for example, a vendor is selling part of his garden. Having agreed what to sell, the vendor could discover that he is losing a treasured tree and decide to redefine the boundary. This must be thrashed out before contracts are exchanged and could hold up the sale.

You normally pay a deposit on exchange of contracts, usually 10 per cent of the agreed price, which is not repayable if you fail to complete the purchase. The completion date is fixed at exchange of contracts and is usually two to four weeks after exchange, although anything from two days to two months would not be uncommon. Between exchange of contracts and completion, the solicitors complete the formalities and arrange for the money to be transferred. Where you take out a mortgage to buy the plot, your solicitor liaises with the bank or building society. The time between exchange and completion gives you the chance to finalise plans, deal with planning permission or to get ready to start building. Whether to make any commitments during this period, such as ordering a kit house, is for you

and your solicitor to decide. The plot only becomes yours after completion. Before that there is always a risk that the sale might not go through. You can sue a vendor for breach of contract and claim any losses you incur, but this is time-consuming, costly and fruitless if he does not have any money. To be safe do not commit any significant amounts of money towards your project, prior to completion, without consulting your solicitor first.

CONTRACTS

The most common type of contract is one that simply records the sale of a plot by one party to another, subject of course to payment. This is known as an outright purchase, and from a vendor's point of view is usually the best way to sell a plot. However, a purchaser might be prepared to buy a plot, but is unwilling to do so unless some other matter is resolved first, like a grant of planning permission. In these circumstances, a conditional contract is often a useful way forward. Conditional contracts are typically used where:

◆ There is outline planning permission but the buyer wants detailed permission before finally committing himself.
◆ The buyer wants a different planning permission.
◆ Planning permission has not been given and the vendor is unwilling or unable to spend money to get it.
◆ A legal matter needs to be resolved, such as a right of way to be negotiated or a restrictive covenant to be overcome.
◆ There is a physical obstacle to overcome, such as the means of drainage to be resolved or sight lines to be improved at the access.

FIGURE 17.3 Example memorandum of sale

MEMORANDUM OF SALE

Re: the proposed sale of: Plot adjoining 22 Highfield Avenue, Trant

                                                    SUBJECT TO CONTRACT

Vendor: JB Builders Ltd, The Forge, High Street, Trant

Solicitor: Finch, Wilson and Co, 47 East Row, Bantley
                         For the attention of Mr C Nyman

Purchaser: Mr and Mrs H Longford, 87 Harding Road, Copton

Solicitor: Beason Birch, 32, High Street, Songton
                         For the attention of Ms J West

Price agreed: £60,000 (sixty thousand pounds) subject to contract

Deposit held: N/A

Tenure: Freehold

Finance/Mortgage: N/A

Local Authority: Trant Borough Council, Town Hall, North Road, Trant

Remarks and Special Conditions:
The Purchaser will be responsible for fencing the plot, details to be approved by the Vendor

A copy of this memorandum has been sent to both parties and their respective Solicitors

Signed on behalf of
Hallingtons, Estate Agents:

B J Metcalfe

B J Metcalfe ARICS
Date: 26th September 1998

The purpose of the conditional contract is to give you security while you spend time and money on the plot or work on a problem that has to be resolved. Strictly speaking, what is often called a conditional contract is actually a contract subject to conditions. Leave these legal niceties to your solicitor. The important point here is that you should have a contract, albeit with conditions attached, and not an agreement to enter a contract if certain conditions are fulfilled. The latter is a conditional offer and you could spend hundreds of pounds getting planning permission only for the vendor to sell to someone else. Your solicitor deals with the detail of a conditional contract.

Where a contract is conditional on planning permission, there are important points to check:

◆ Is the contract subject to you obtaining full or outline planning permission?
◆ If permission is granted subject to planning conditions, what planning conditions would be unacceptable?
◆ If the council resolves to grant planning permission subject to a legal agreement, what terms or requirements in such an agreement would be unacceptable?
◆ If planning permission is refused, does the contract allow for an appeal?
◆ If an appeal is dismissed, does the contract allow for the submission of a new scheme?
◆ Where the vendor has a mortgage, does he have the permission of the building society to enter into the contract?

You and your solicitor must consider these possibilities carefully to avoid becoming committed to buy a plot when planning permission is given, only to find that you are unable to build the house that you want because of some defect in the permission.

So far we have looked at conditional contracts from a buyer's point of view, but these contracts must be negotiated with the vendor. He probably wants a quick completion and might not be willing to wait while you indulge in lengthy planning battles over some design feature of your dream house that has little bearing on the plot value. The vendor could try to restrict the time allowed to get your permission and insist on a cut-off date to stop matters dragging on, after which the contract ends. Remember that the whole purpose of the conditional contract is to give you time to sort out planning or other matters. Allow at least five months to gain planning permission; if the vendor will not give you adequate time, do not enter into the contract.

An option to buy a plot, as the name suggests, is a right to buy a plot at some future date. Options are widely used by developers who buy an option on a piece of land with potential, and then try to get planning permission on it. An option involves paying a sum now for the right to buy within a certain number of years, either for a fixed amount or for a percentage of the open market value when the option is exercised. This is a way to stop others buying a plot while you work on it or decide whether to go ahead and buy it. To a landowner, an option can be attractive as it involves receiving some immediate cash while someone else works to make his land more valuable. Consider an option where:

◆ You find a perfect site, but are not in a position to buy straight away.
◆ You are not sure that you can get planning permission for the house you want to build.

◆ You want to secure one or more sites for future projects.

What you pay for an option, and then for the plot itself, is a matter for negotiation and agreement between the parties. The level depends partly on the amount of down payment at the start, and partly on the degree of risk and amount of work to be shouldered by the purchaser. If you agree to pay a percentage of the market value, this would normally be in the region of 70-85 per cent. You must pay something for the option, even if it is just £1, otherwise it will not be legally binding.

In most cases a conditional contract is more suitable for buying a plot than using an option. The main advantage of an option is that you do not have to proceed to buy if you do not want to. If you do consider trying to secure an option on a plot, discuss it with your solicitor who will need to draft a suitable option agreement. Key points to be covered are:

◆ The sum to be paid.
◆ The duration of the option.
◆ The steps to be taken to obtain planning permission.
◆ The price to be paid for the land or how it is to be calculated.
◆ Provisions in the case of disputes.

PURCHASE AND TAKING POSSESSION

After exchange of contracts, the purchase is in the hands of your solicitor or conveyancer and progress to completion should be a formality. But things can go wrong even at this late stage. Your solicitor could still find defects in the vendor's ownership, for example part of the access could turn out to be in private ownership and not part of the adopted highway, or a registered title incorrectly registered. Ask your solicitor to keep you informed, especially of problems that arise. Do not accept legal jargon, but get explanations in terms that you understand. Ask about the implications of any problems and how long they will take to resolve. Where questions of ownership arise that could affect your ability to build on the plot, resolve them prior to completion. If a query about, say, the exact position of a rear boundary does not fundamentally affect your plans for the plot, proceed with the purchase, but do not do this unless your solicitor has clearly explained any risks involved.

Occasionally a buyer is unable to complete the purchase and has to default on the contract. You not only risk losing your deposit, but also risk further claims from the vendor. Again, discuss any difficulties you have with your solicitor.

Completion of the purchase allows you to take possession of the plot. If you think security could be a problem, arrange for some form of fencing on completion day or before you store materials on the plot. As soon as you purchase a plot you need to take out public liability insurance. If your soil engineer digs a hole to test ground conditions and a trespasser falls in and is injured, you are liable.

When you take possession, you are limited in what you can do without planning permission. If you already have detailed planning permission and building regulations approval, you can go ahead and build. If you do not have planning permission or only have an outline permission, you should not start work. If you do, you might upset the council and neighbours, which might not help your cause when you make a detailed planning application.

Having planning permission to build a new home does not automatically mean that you can live in a caravan or mobile home on the plot, although this is a grey area in planning. The basic rule is that you need separate permission to live in a caravan or mobile home on the plot, unless you are fully employed in the construction of the house. Councils stopped people living in caravans on site where:

◆ A selfbuilder, because of injury, had to bring in sub-contractors to complete the building.
◆ An owner travelled to his plot every weekend to build a retirement home; because he had a full-time job

elsewhere, he was not 'employed', in building the house.
◆ A family converting a barn stopped building for financial reasons and were not then 'employed' on the building as no work was taking place.

This does not mean you have to lay every brick yourself; you can satisfy the tests by having a managerial role in the building. If you are not going to be fully employed in the building of your home, you can speak to a planning officer at the district council about living in a caravan on site. In practice, it is unlikely that the council would be concerned about the temporary siting of a caravan. Even if it was, the chances are that you would have finished building and moved into the house before the council came to take action to remove the caravan.

In areas and times of high demand, good plots can attract a dozen or more firm offers. The buyers who succeed are well prepared, act quickly and read the state of the market accurately to outbid their rivals.

We saw earlier how to assess and value a plot. During the course of that process you will probably have spoken to the vendor's agents; if not, contact them as soon as you think a particular plot is right for you. Say that you are about to make an offer, that your finance is in place and that your solicitor is geared up for an early exchange of contracts. Ideally, have a letter from your lender or bank confirming that funds are available. Ask about other interested buyers and whether any offers have been made, at what level, and when a decision is likely. Find out how the agents intend to proceed and whether there would be an opportunity to review your offer if there are other offers at the same or a higher level.

Make your offer as soon as you have all your information to hand, but do not recklessly throw in a figure with a view to adjusting it later, as this would not impress the agents or vendor and could spoil your chances. If you are still waiting for information which is delaying your offer, tell the vendor's agents. Provided you convince them that you are a serious buyer, they are likely to advise the vendor to delay a decision until your offer is in.

Judging the right level for your offer is not usually difficult if, during your plot finding and valuing, you gain a clear picture of the local plot market using the valuation methods suggested earlier (see Chapter 15). You should know the asking price, market value, what you would like to pay and what is the most you could pay. In a busy market do not try to get away with too low a figure. If several offers are made and yours is one of the

lowest, you might not get a chance to increase your figure. In a slow market, and particularly if there is little, or no, competition, start with a low offer, especially if the plot has been on the market for any length of time. Look at the chances of finding another plot if you fail to buy this one and think about whether this plot is right and you really want to buy it. Ultimately, only you can balance all the factors and make the decision.

Making an offer is a simple process: telephone the vendor's agents and tell them what figure you are offering and that you will confirm it in writing. They are likely to ask whether you have a house to sell, who your lender is, what you intend to build and who your solicitor is. Include these details in your letter, as shown in Figure 18.1. Do not make your offer subject to any other, for example '£500 more than the highest'; this is extremely reckless. Your offer should clearly state if it is conditional - dependent on planning permission for example - or whether you want to enter into a conditional contract.

Developers sometimes include uplift clauses in offers, allowing for an additional amount to be paid if they get a better planning permission or a higher price than expected when they sell the finished house. These clauses make offers more attractive to vendors, but unless you intend to sell quickly, an uplift clause based on a sale price is not appropriate. Uplift clauses are written into contracts and need to be discussed with your solicitor.

NEGOTIATING

Once an offer is made it may be accepted outright, but sometimes there is a period of negotiation due to competing offers or because your offer simply falls below the

FIGURE 18.1 Letter making an offer for a plot

John and Mary Wright
43, Nelson Avenue
Fairnborough
Hunts

Benfield, Snetterton and Partners
Estate Agents
41, The Chase
Stollington
Hunts   12th January
1999

For the attention of Harry Stagnorth

Dear Sirs,

Re: Plot at 'Graftons', The Avenue, Stollington

I refer to my recent telephone conversation with Mr Stagnorth and now confirm my offer for this plot of £45,000 (forty five thousand pounds).

I enclose a copy of a letter from my building society confirming the availability of funds for the purchase.

My solicitor is Mr Brian Holmsworth of Jarvis Holmsworth, 22 The Chase, Stollington.

If this offer is accepted, my solicitor will respond quickly to receipt of a draft contract, with a view to an early exchange and completion.

Yours faithfully

John Wright

John Wright

An example of a letter making an offer for a plot. This letter confirms the essential ingredients of an offer: the amount, the funds, and the intention to go ahead without delay.

vendor's expectations. In the latter case the agent usually knows the figure at which the vendor would sell and might tell you the figure or ask you to increase your offer. If yours is the only offer, you are in a strong position, but the vendor might begin a further round of advertising and marketing to drum up a better figure. However, the agents will not relish this prospect as it will mean more work for the same commission. If your figures allow for an increase and the price still appears to be at a reasonable market level, by all means make a revised offer. Sound out the agents carefully before you do this and, if you sense that the vendor is in a hurry to sell, try adding the incentive of a fast exchange of contracts and completion to your original offer. Make sure your solicitor knows what you are offering. If he is just starting his annual holiday, you could have problems delivering your extra-quick purchase.

Where there are competing offers, the sale might go in a number of different ways. Agents monitor the level of interest in a plot, record who offers what and when and report regularly to their client, the vendor. The sample diary extract in Figure 18.2 shows how agents might record the offers received on a plot. Where more than one offer is made, they must decide which to advise their client to accept. The vendor is interested primarily in the amount of money and the certainty of the buyer completing the sale. You must make sure that the agent has confidence in your ability to go ahead. You will probably meet the agent once or twice or possibly only speak to him on the telephone. From these fleeting communications, the agent will sum you up. This is not a sophisticated process: you will be seen as either a genuine purchaser or a time waster. Those in the latter category face an uphill struggle in any negotiations and risk being excluded

altogether. The secret in dealing with agents is to be well-prepared and businesslike, as this gives the right message. If your message is that you are thinking about building your own home one day, but have not thought much about it, you are giving the wrong signals.

Once you make an offer for a plot, there is an uncertain stage before it is accepted, lasting hours or weeks. Negotiations can be complex, especially when a number of people all want the same plot and events can take a number of courses:

◆ There is a clear winner whose offer is accepted.
◆ The offers are close and all bidders, or the top two or three, are invited to make revised offers.
◆ An informal tender is held, where best and final offers are invited by a certain date.
◆ A Dutch auction is held.
◆ A contracts race takes place.

Where you are invited to reconsider your offer, you must decide how badly you want the plot, and how close to your maximum figure you are prepared to go. Everyone likes a bargain but, where there is competition, it might take your best offer to secure the plot. Get as much information as you can from the agents about other offers and the vendor's expectations. Agents vary in helpfulness, but try asking their advice on the right level to offer. Judge their comments against your knowledge of the plot market. Do not be tempted to go over your maximum figure.

INFORMAL TENDERS

Informal tenders are held where there are several offers but no obvious winner has emerged. This could follow the first round of offers or be used after revised offers have been made. The agents invite buyers to make their best and final offers, in writing, by a given time and date. The tender is described as 'informal' because the vendor does not have to accept the highest, or any, offer and acceptance does not immediately create a binding contract. From a purchaser's point of view an informal tender is something of a shot in the dark. It is your best offer against someone else's. You must simply go in as high as you can, bearing in mind your budget. Find out as much as you can about the competition. Developers, builders and speculators make offers that are not too far from market value. Private individuals are less predictable. If the plot is exceptional in some way, offers are sometimes made well above the apparent value of the plot.

Send your written offer in response to an informal tender to the agents in good time before the close of the tender period, and check that it has arrived. If you are unhappy with the way the sale is being handled, or are suspicious about the relationship between other buyers and the agents, deliver your offer personally just before the time when the tender closes. Sometimes agents provide a form and envelope for your tender; if not, clearly mark the outside of the envelope, otherwise it could be opened accidentally before the proper time. Make sure that your tender gives all the information required by the agents, which might include the name and address of your solicitor or conveyancer and possibly a financial reference. Even if these are not asked for, there is nothing to lose in supplying them anyway. Sometimes offers are made of a sum like £50,001, in the hope of beating another's of £50,000, but it is generally better to work in units of at least £100.

Once an informal tender has been held it is highly unlikely that any further negotiation will take place. The successful bidder is informed, and a memorandum of sale is drawn up and the sale goes ahead.

DUTCH AUCTIONS

Dutch auction is the name usually given to what is actually a private auction. Bidders are told the highest bid and invited to bid against each other. A real Dutch auction is actually an auction where the price starts high and falls slowly until a buyer makes the one and only successful bid, and is not a practice used in Britain. Despite this, the misuse of the name is widespread and, for convenience, we will continue to misuse it here. Curiously, builders and developers often refuse to take part in a Dutch auction when asked to review their offers, because vendors might try to push up the bidding, and since negotiations are held in private, there is scope for sharp practice. The advantage of a Dutch auction is that offers are in the open and negotiations which involve naming other bids sometimes mean you can end by paying less than your maximum figure.

CONTRACTS RACES

When two or more acceptable offers are made, a vendor can select the successful buyer through a contracts race, which involves his solicitor issuing draft contracts to the bidders and the first to exchange contracts gets the plot. If a vendor suggests a contracts race, discuss this immediately with your solicitor. You must understand any risks involved in speeding matters up and be prepared to pay abortive fees if you lose. If you have doubts about a contracts race, and especially if you do not want to write off legal fees, do not enter.

FIGURE 18.2 Estate agent's file notes on a plot sale

```
PLOT:    PINE TREE LANE
CLIENT: PETER AND SARAH MATHERSON
```

21/2/98 - Clients confirm instructions to market plot and approve
particulars.
'For Sale' board arranged, adverts placed.

1/3/98 - Telephone call: Mr D Bromley, 14 Swinbourne Avenue,
Handle, 0654 778321, made an offer £40,000, but has a house to sell
so is not ready to go ahead with purchase immediately.

3/3/98 - John Marlborough, Marlborough Developments called into the
office, made an offer £40,000 with early exchange of contracts,
confirmed they would give us the finished house to sell.

3/3/98 - Mrs A Bingham called in, made offer of £39,500, and gave
written confirmation of offer with her financial references, her
solicitors are Wilkins & Partners, can buy quickly.

10/3/98 - Telephone call: John Marlborough, asking if his offer is
OK, asked if I am free for lunch next Friday.

15/3/98 Telephone call: Richard Parks, Rocks House, Brinkley 0861
439117, tentative offer of £36,500, he is still talking to planning
officers about the plot and hopes his finance will be in place next
week so he can confirm his offer. Sounds a bit vague.

18/3/98 Report to clients: recommend they accept Marlborough
Developments' offer, as is the highest and is reliable.
Clients want us to ask for 'best and final' offers.
Recommend we leave out Mr Bromley as he has a house to sell and
Richard Parks as he has not come up with a firm offer.
Agree to ask Marlborough Developments and Mrs Bingham for their best
offers by 25th.
Notify Bromley and Parks they have been unsuccessful.

23/3/98 - Telephone call: John Marlborough, he will increase his
offer, and was fishing for clues on what price would get him the
plot.

25/3/98 - Offers made: Mrs Bingham £44,000, with early exchange.
John Marlborough £42,500, with early exchange.
Telephone clients: both offers are certainties, clients to take the
highest offer.

Put sale in hand to Mrs Bingham.
Memorandum of sale completed and sent.
John Marlborough notified he was unsuccessful.

*These notes show how an agent might react to offers being made for a plot.
Approaches will be varied. In this case, with a little prompting from his clients, the
agent has got it right. Joan Bingham was lucky to buy this plot, she nearly lost out to
the developer by making an initial offer that was too low. The developer had made all
the right moves but when it came to best offers he could not top the private individual.
J Bromley made an offer at the right level, but without finance ready to go, his offer
was as good as worthless. Richard Parks' offer was too low and too vague.*

Making an Offer and Negotiation

CHANGING YOUR OFFER

After your offer is accepted and before you exchange contracts, you might come across a problem that means you are no longer willing to pay the agreed price. The scope for reducing your offer and still buying the plot depends largely on whether the reason for the reduction is personal to you, such as problems with finance, or applies to any purchaser, such as the need for special foundations. Personal reasons will not sway the vendor, unless you are the only buyer in a very quiet market. In these circumstances you might try lowering your offer, especially if you can sweeten the pill with an early date for exchange and completion. In a busy market, reducing your offer for personal reasons is likely to lose you the plot.

If you have good reasons that would apply to any purchaser, put the facts together before speaking to the agents. For example, if you discover an unmarked private sewer across the plot that must be diverted before building takes place, get a written quote for the work and then speak to the vendor or agents. Unless several thousand pounds is involved, the vendor would probably expect you to bear the extra cost. If the sum is significant and affects the plot's value, decide whether you can pay some part of it. Whatever the state of the market, approach reducing your offer carefully; by this stage you have put a good deal of effort into buying the plot and tact and some flexibility could help you keep it.

As we have seen, exchange of contracts is a legally binding agreement to buy. Do not sign the contract until you are satisfied with the results of all your investigations. It is not unusual for exchange of contracts to be delayed by a few days or even weeks, while problems are sorted out. Keep the agents informed of any difficulties and be as precise as you can about the problem and how long it will take to sort out. Provided you maintain the agents' confidence in your ability and intention to go ahead, a delay in signing contracts should not jeopardise your purchase.

GAZUMPING

Gazumping means that a vendor agrees a sale with one person, but before contracts are exchanged, accepts a higher offer from someone else. He is legally entitled to do this, despite any moral arguments against it. Some vendors, for example trustees or liquidators, are legally bound to consider any higher offer they get. Agents have a legal duty to their client, the vendor, to pass on offers even after a sale is agreed. You are particularly at risk of being gazumped if, for whatever reason, the vendor is not confident in your ability to complete the sale. This lack of confidence usually manifests itself in continued marketing after the sale has been agreed. Check that any 'for sale' board is replaced by a 'sold subject to contract' sign, and that all advertising stops. If you are gazumped, decide whether it is worth making a higher offer or matching the other offer. Where your purchase is well under way, the vendor is likely to stick with you rather than start again from scratch.

Otherwise reaffirm to the agents that you remain interested in the plot, that your solicitor can act quickly and that your offer remains on the table. Ask the agents to let you know if the other purchaser does not complete. If the first purchaser drops out, there is then a good chance that your offer will be snapped up without further marketing of the plot. Most sales do go ahead though, so keep looking for another plot.

Sales of plots by auction are more common in England and Wales than in Scotland, and almost unheard of in Northern Ireland. They are well worth investigating, however, especially if you are looking for a bargain. There are differences between sale by auction and sale by private treaty and you must be clear about these before bidding for a plot at auction.

The first and most important point to understand about buying a plot by auction is that the fall of the auctioneer's hammer creates a binding contract. This equates to exchange of contracts in a sale by private treaty. Once the hammer has fallen, the sale progresses to completion in the normal way. Auction procedure is shown in Figure 19.1.

Before bidding at an auction, adequate preparation is essential. Your solicitor must have carried out all the searches and investigations of the title. Only then can you buy with confidence. Your investigations will be simplified as both the selling agent and the vendor's solicitors anticipate enquiries and should be geared up to answer them. Auction particulars are more detailed than ordinary sales particulars, including addresses of local councils and service authorities and information about easements and covenants. Particulars include a memorandum of sale and special conditions of sale (see Figure 19.2). The memorandum is for the successful buyer to sign as proof of purchase. The special conditions of sale set out details of the title and any restrictions; other documents, like the planning permission, should be available from the agent.

Tell your solicitors or conveyancers as soon as you are certain that you want to bid. They must liaise with the vendor's solicitors and carry out the necessary searches. You also need to make sure that your finance is in place. Even though, at this stage, you do not know whether you will be successful in buying the plot, you still have to pay the solicitor and give a good deal of time and effort to your research. Do not think about bidding at auction unless you are certain that the plot is right for you. Where time is short or assessing the plot is complex, get professional help from a firm of surveyors. Explain the time pressures and make it absolutely clear what you need from them.

There is nothing to stop you making an offer for a plot before the auction. Because of the costs agents incur when arranging an auction (advertising, hire of hall, etc.), they may be reluctant to entertain early offers but are, nevertheless, obliged to pass them on to their clients, unless given specific instructions to the contrary. Particulars marked 'for sale by auction unless previously sold', suggest a willingness, even an intention, to sell before the auction. An early offer has the disadvantage of indicating the amount that you are likely to bid at the auction, and the vendor might adjust the reserve price. If you want to make an offer before the auction, do so as soon as the agents are instructed to sell. At this point, the agents have not committed much time to arranging the auction and so might recommend the vendor to accept an early offer. You can put forward an offer at any time up to and including the day of the auction. The agents should have some idea of how many people are likely to bid and if there are very few, your offer might succeed.

An auction is often a last resort method of selling a plot, so you should first find out whether there is a problem and why any previous attempts to sell it were unsuccessful. Not all plots sold in this way have something

FIGURE 19.1 Auction sale procedure

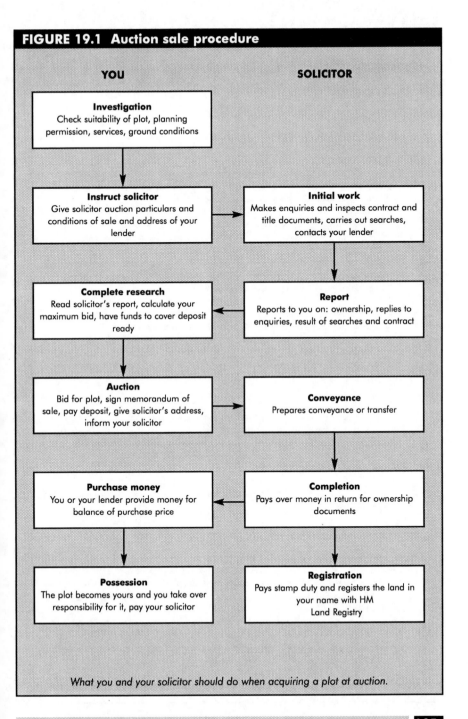

YOU

SOLICITOR

Investigation
Check suitability of plot, planning permission, services, ground conditions

Instruct solicitor
Give solicitor auction particulars and conditions of sale and address of your lender

Initial work
Makes enquiries and inspects contract and title documents, carries out searches, contacts your lender

Complete research
Read solicitor's report, calculate your maximum bid, have funds to cover deposit ready

Report
Reports to you on: ownership, replies to enquiries, result of searches and contract

Auction
Bid for plot, sign memorandum of sale, pay deposit, give solicitor's address, inform your solicitor

Conveyance
Prepares conveyance or transfer

Purchase money
You or your lender provide money for balance of purchase price

Completion
Pays over money in return for ownership documents

Possession
The plot becomes yours and you take over responsibility for it, pay your solicitor

Registration
Pays stamp duty and registers the land in your name with HM Land Registry

What you and your solicitor should do when acquiring a plot at auction.

FIGURE 19.2 Example conditions of sale attached to auction particulars

GENERAL CONDITIONS OF SALE

1. The Vendor's solicitors are Messrs Hunt and Stevens of 49, Church Road, Hinchley, Muddlesex, telephone 01743 094635.

2. (a) The property is sold subject to the following conditions and to the conditions known as the National Conditions of Sale so far as the latter conditions are not inconsistent with these general and special conditions which are to prevail in case of any conflict.

   (b) The prescribed rate of interest referred to in condition (4) of the National Conditions of Sale shall be 5% above the minimum lending rate of National Westminster Bank for the time being.

   (c) A copy of the said conditions may be inspected at the offices of the auctioneers or of the solicitors for the Vendors on any day during business hours and in the sale room immediately before the sale and the purchaser shall be deemed to have full knowledge thereof.

3. Immediately following the sale the purchaser will pay a deposit of 10% of the purchase money to the auctioneers as stakeholders and shall sign the agreement hereinafter appearing.

4. Unless otherwise stated the sale is subject to a reserve price and the vendors reserve the right to bid themselves or through their agents at the auction and to sell all or any part of the property by private treaty prior to the auction.

5. Notwithstanding anything in these conditions or in the particulars of sale no representation, warranty or condition whatsoever shall be made or implied howsoever arising either as to the state or condition of the property or any part thereof or as to whether the same is subject to any resolutions, schemes, development orders, notices or proposals of any sort whatsoever and the purchaser shall be deemed to purchase in all respects subject thereto and shall not be entitled to raise any requisition in respect thereof.

6. The auctioneers reserve the right (without assigning any reason therefore) in their sole absolute discretion to refuse to accept a bid.

SPECIAL CONDITIONS OF SALE

1. Vacant possession shall be given on completion.
2. Completion shall take place on the 13th day of May, 1998, at the office of the Vendor's solicitor.
3. Title shall commence with a Conveyance on sale dated 15th June 1947, and made between Richard Stanley Waters and William James Hollis and the prior title shall in no circumstances be required or investigated.
4. The property is sold subject to but with the benefit of the provisions of a Deed of Grant dated 9th January, 1984 whereby a right of way over the access road was granted by the owner or owners for the time being of Honeywood Cottage being the property immediately to the north. A copy of this Deed is available for inspection at the office of the auctioneers and of the Vendor's solicitors.

FIGURE 19.3 Plot for sale at auction

Good building plots - level, well-fenced, spacious, with an existing access and in a select area - are few and far between. So much so that the highest figure a buyer would pay is not known. Competition between buyers is likely to be very strong and so these plots are often put into auctions to get the maximum price.

wrong with them. Trustees frequently sell properties at auctions, indicated in the particulars by a phrase like 'to be sold by order of trustees or executors'. Some plots are so special that their values are hard to predict and they are put into auctions to get the highest possible price through competitive bidding. In the latter cases, the plot normally goes to the auction no matter what offers are made beforehand.

There is a mystique surrounding auctions, but the procedure for selling a plot is straightforward and the proceedings are not difficult to follow. If the prospect of bidding alarms you, attend another auction to see at first hand how it is done or employ someone to bid for you. You do not need special inside knowledge to be able to buy a plot at auction. The auctioneer does not set out at an incoherent gabble and bidding is usually made by clearly raising a hand. The auctioneer responds by repeating the figure bid before going on to seek the next bid.

In the auction room, there might be many people present. Not all will be buyers: some could be members of the auctioneer's staff, drafted in to create a busy atmosphere; other buyers have their solicitors or other professionals with them; inquisitive locals and neighbours also attend. A large crowd can disguise only a few genuine purchasers.

When the auction begins, the auctioneer

first explains who he is and introduces the vendor's solicitor. As each property, or lot, comes up, the auctioneer gives a brief description and mentions any key documents, like the planning permission, and points out items in the special conditions of sale, such as a restrictive covenant or right of way across the plot. The auctioneer states when completion is to take place and asks for any questions. Do not be dismayed if at this point someone stands up and asks loudly about some problem with the site, like a public footpath across it. If your thorough investigations have not uncovered any problems, it is probably a buyer's ploy to discourage others from bidding. Where buyers make a public misrepresentation about a plot and then succeed in the auction, their contract could be void. Even if they do not succeed, they could still be liable for damages. Do not let this deter you from asking a genuine question, however.

The bidding is started by the auctioneer naming a figure, which might be low to encourage bidding, or high, but then rapidly reduced, to give the impression that a bargain is to be had. Vendors can reserve the right to bid themselves and in practice this usually means that the auctioneer bids on their behalf, taking imaginary bids or bids 'off the wall' as it is known. The particulars state whether a vendor reserves the right to bid. Bidding goes on until the reserve price is reached. This is the minimum sale price which the vendor and auctioneer agree before the auction. If bids fail to reach this level, the lot is withdrawn. Once bids reach the reserve price, the auctioneer says that the lot 'is to be sold' or that bids are 'in the room'. Where bidding is brisk, the auctioneer might delay making this announcement until there is a pause, when it can help to get bidding moving again.

Once you know that the reserve has been reached, and thus the plot will be sold, your task is to secure it at the best possible figure. Keep in mind both the highest figure you can pay and your estimate of market value. You must judge exactly how far you are prepared to go. If bidding is moving in stages of £1,000 and you are within £3,000 or £4,000 of your limit, slow your bids right down. The auctioneer can tell when buyers are nearing their ceiling figures and might then ask for bids of, say, £500. If he does not, you can make such a bid yourself, by naming a figure as opposed to signalling your agreement to the one the auctioneer is seeking. The auctioneer might not accept the bid and by doing this you send a clear signal to other bidders that you are reaching your limit. If you accidentally make a bid beyond your limit, you can withdraw it before the fall of the hammer. Do not get carried away. Remember that, if the hammer falls after your bid, you are legally bound to buy.

If you are successful, you will sign a memorandum of sale and pay a deposit, usually 10 per cent of the sale figure. You will be asked where copies of the title deeds should be sent, so have your solicitor's name and address with you.

When a plot fails to reach its reserve, you can still try to buy it after the auction. Where bidding stops just short of the reserve, the vendor might negotiate, if he has set his figure too high. Tell the auctioneer that you want to make an offer. If the plot is bought after the auction, you can sign the memorandum of sale and pay the deposit as if the deal had been done in the auction.

In England, Wales and Northern Ireland, formal tenders are rarely used to sell single plots, but in Scotland tenders are the normal way of buying and selling plots and houses. In this chapter we first examine the special features of buying land in Scotland and then look at buying by formal tender generally.

BUYING A PLOT IN SCOTLAND

Scotland has a different legal system from the rest of Britain and different procedures for conveyancing and land registration, so you must use a solicitor who is a member of the Scottish Law Society. Scottish solicitors are more active in the property market than their counterparts elsewhere in Britain and act as both legal and property advisers.

When plots are put up for sale, the normal procedure is for offers to be invited over a given figure, which really does mean over, say, 10 - 15 per cent, or even more in a rising market. A closing date is given for offers to be made.

When you find a plot you want to buy, consult your solicitors about what would be the right offer. They will advise on value, and draft and submit the offer on your behalf. An offer is made as a sealed bid which, if accepted by the vendor, is termed conclusion of missives. This creates a binding contract and the sale moves ahead quickly with completion taking place in as little as a week. This is largely due to the relative simplicity of making title searches in Scotland, where there is a central register of property transactions.

Not all plot sales in Scotland are conducted by sealed bids, nor is every property sold by solicitors. Estate agents are active in commercial and agricultural property and increasingly in the residential market too. Sales of land do take place by private treaty. If you are in any doubt about the method of sale, ask the agent or solicitor selling the plot, or take advice from your own solicitor. Because offers can be binding when accepted, and sales move quickly, you must make all your investigations into the plot before you commit yourself to buy.

FORMAL TENDERS

We have already looked at the use of informal tenders as a way of putting forward offers before contracts are agreed and signed. A formal tender is an offer to buy a plot which, if accepted, results in a binding contract. This method of sale favours vendors, as there is no scope for negotiation, rather than buyers, who incur legal and other costs in preparing their bid regardless of the outcome. For these reasons, formal tenders are normally used only in busy market conditions. The main stages are set out in Figure 20.1.

Preparing for a tender is the same as preparing for an auction. Tender particulars and conditions of sale received from the selling agent give the time and place for submitting your tender and you should pass this on to your solicitor immediately. All site investigations, enquiries and legal searches need to be carried out before your tender is submitted. Finance must be in place and a deposit cheque (normally for 10 per cent of your tender figure) has to be included with your tender. Read the conditions of sale carefully as they include conditions for tendering, and probably rule out offers made subject to planning or subject to anything else. If you have doubts about any aspects of the plot, do not submit a tender.

When deciding on a figure for your tender, remember that this is your one and only bid, so make your best offer. Try to get an indication from the vendor's agents of what

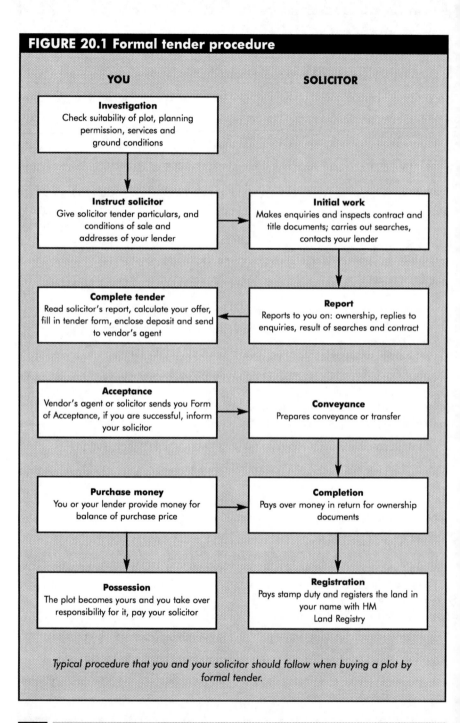

FIGURE 20.1 Formal tender procedure

YOU

SOLICITOR

Investigation
Check suitability of plot, planning permission, services and ground conditions

Instruct solicitor
Give solicitor tender particulars, and conditions of sale and addresses of your lender

Initial work
Makes enquiries and inspects contract and title documents; carries out searches, contacts your lender

Complete tender
Read solicitor's report, calculate your offer, fill in tender form, enclose deposit and send to vendor's agent

Report
Reports to you on: ownership, replies to enquiries, result of searches and contract

Acceptance
Vendor's agent or solicitor sends you Form of Acceptance, if you are successful, inform your solicitor

Conveyance
Prepares conveyance or transfer

Purchase money
You or your lender provide money for balance of purchase price

Completion
Pays over money in return for ownership documents

Possession
The plot becomes yours and you take over responsibility for it, pay your solicitor

Registration
Pays stamp duty and registers the land in your name with HM Land Registry

Typical procedure that you and your solicitor should follow when buying a plot by formal tender.

FIGURE 20.2 Example form of tender sent to a prospective plot buyer

FORM OF TENDER

The Conditions of Tender and Sale should be read before completion and submission of this Form.

Tender to purchase the freehold land and buildings at London Road, Bankley, in the County of Midshire ('the property') in accordance with the conditions of Tender and Sale annexed hereto,

TO: Hilltop Farms Limited
            c/o Messrs Griffin Jones and Partners
            Prospect House
            High Street
            Kimbleton
            Midshire KM3 9FW

I/WE ..... *Mr and Mrs K R Jones* .....

of ..... *47 Albion Street* .....

..... *Sewal Midshire* .....

hereby offer to purchase the Property from Hilltop Farms Limited for the sum of *THIRTY SIX THOUSAND AND FIVE HUNDRED* POUNDS (*£36,500*) and agree that this Form of Tender with written notice of acceptance signed on behalf of Hilltop Farms Limited and despatched by recorded delivery post on or before the 5th day of August 1998 to me/us at my/our above mentioned address shall form a binding contract and subject to the Conditions of Tender and Sale. A Bankers Draft in favour of Fripp, Holdsworth and Barrington for ten per centum of the sum tendered is enclosed.

Dated this *1st*   day of *May 1998*

Signature/Signatures   *K R Jones*

Address of Agent or of Principal where different from above

.....

Name and Address of Tenderer's Solicitors
DUNN CELMONT & LORD, EVANS PLACE, KIMBLETON .....

NOTES:
When submitting this Form of Tender, please ensure you comply with the Conditions of Tender, that the form is correctly filled in, and the Bankers Draft is in the right amount and payable to the Vendor's Solicitor. Do not submit the Tender unless you are certain you can proceed with the purchase, if successful.

they think the market value is and what level the vendor might accept. There is little point in attempting to save money by putting in a figure below your best, merely because the vendor's agents claim that a lower figure might be acceptable. Get professional help if you are determined to buy the plot but do not have enough time to carry out the necessary research thoroughly. When you fill in the tender document make sure that all the details are correct and double check that everything is presented in the way specified, as failure to do this can invalidate your tender (see Figure 20.2). Enclose your deposit cheque correctly filled in, signed and dated. Tender particulars state where to send your tender, usually to either the vendor's agents or solicitors. There might be instructions on how to mark the envelope, or even a special envelope provided, but if not, mark it 'Tender Documents' and the name of the property.

Developers often time the submission of their tenders carefully and some send them by messenger, who loiters outside the agents' office until five minutes before the time limit. This is done to minimise the risk of sharp practice, as a dishonest agent could open tenders early and pass on information to another buyer. If you want to be safe, you could deliver the tender yourself, on the morning of the tender date; otherwise send it by registered mail and telephone to check that it has arrived.

If you are successful in your tender, the agents will let you know that your tender has been accepted, subject to clearance of your deposit cheque. A formal notice is sent by the vendor's solicitors and the purchase goes on to completion in the normal way. If you are unsuccessful, you will be informed and your deposit cheque returned. You will no doubt be interested in the amount of the successful tender, but the agents are unlikely to tell you. They will normally say how many tenders there were and roughly where you came in the pecking order. This is useful information as it gives you a clearer picture of the level of competition for the type of plot you are seeking.

BUYING YOUR PLOT - CHECK LIST

◆ Be ready to act quickly, once you find a plot you want to buy; get a letter from your lender or bank confirming availability of funds.

◆ Discuss the plot with the vendor/agents and make your offer in writing.

◆ Get answers to all your queries before you exchange contracts.

◆ Before bidding for a plot at an auction or submitting a tender, your solicitor must have checked ownership documents and you must be satisfied that you can build your house on it.

◆ Check that sale plans agree with the plot boundaries on the ground and get the plot pegged out if necessary.

◆ Make sure you understand fully all the implications of a conditional contract.

◆ Stay in touch with the vendor/agents throughout the purchase.

◆ When you buy a plot, do not start work on site until you have detailed planning permission and Building Regulations approval.

Successfully finding and buying a plot of land to build your house on, or a property to convert, is as much about your personal qualities as it is about technical knowledge. Persistence, ingenuity, forward planning, flexibility, imagination and bare-faced cheek can all play a vital role in land-finding.

The first five Parts of this book give you the knowledge and information you will need. In the final Part, we see how three couples have put this all together - the challenges they faced, the methods they used and the valuable lessons learned which they want to pass on to you.

SHARON AND GEOFF JONES, SUFFOLK

Sharon and Geoff Jones caught the self build bug many years ago when they visited Home World, in Milton Keynes. But it was not until nearly a decade later that they were in a position to seriously contemplate a self build project of their own.

The first challenge, as is often the case, was finding the right plot. Sharon and Geoff knew they wanted to live in the Bury St Edmonds area, and knew they wanted to build a timber frame home from timber frame home suppliers Medina Gimson. They contacted local estate agents and scoured the local papers regularly. There were plots available, but all seemed either to be too narrow or in odd positions. Their efforts,

Sharon admitted, were not as wholehearted as they could have been. Others seemed to be plot hunting practically full time, and consequently were snapping up the best plots.

Eventually they did locate a likely looking plot but problems soon became evident. Firstly the planning permission required a low ridge line with dormers in the roof, which was not the Jones's first choice of design. Then the plot itself turned out to be an odd shape. A 59 foot frontage quickly narrowed to 44 feet, although this was not immediately obvious from the plans and was only discovered from boundary posts hidden in undergrowth. The final straw was the discovery that the local school was about to close, and a good local school was a priority for their daughter Penny. It was back to plot hunting again.

After a total period of looking for nearly two years, fate intervened. Sharon took a detour on her drive to work to avoid a traffic jam, and spotted an ideal plot. There was, though, one major snag - the for sale board had 'sold' across it. Undeterred, Sharon and Geoff decided to investigate further and returned for a closer look a few days later. This time the for sale board appeared to have gone, only to turn up under leaves behind the hedge. Contacting the Agents, they discovered the sale had fallen through, although the agent was not particularly enthusiastic until they mentioned they were cash purchasers and ready to proceed. Their first offer was accepted.

An early challenge was the need to get planning permission quickly, as the existing permission only had six months left to run. There were some unexpected difficulties. Firstly, an objection to their render and beam finish, on the basis that this was not typical of

FIGURE 21.1 The Jones' site layout

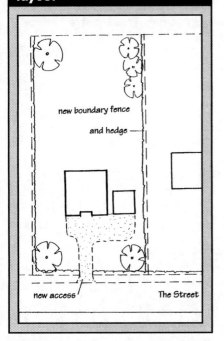

new boundary fence and hedge —

new access

The Street

the village. This was an odd objection, given that many of the houses in the immediate vicinity had exactly the same finish. Then there was some discussion about the distance the house should be from the road, as there was no obvious building line. This was agreed, as was the planners' requirement for a walnut tree to be planted in the back garden. A walnut was specified as apparently one had once stood in a neighbouring garden and the planners thought this was a good opportunity to get a replacement planted. Finally there was much debate as to where the drains should run. The planners were insistent on a position which Geoff considered unsuitable, but, to keep matters moving and secure the permission, Geoff conceded the point. Later, when the trenches were dug, Geoff's point was proven correct and an alternative route had to be found.

The Jones were confident that getting finance for their project would be straightforward. They had bought the plot outright, and the special scheme for self builders offered by their building society had recently been featured in *Build It* magazine. Unfortunately the manager of their local branch appeared neither to have read the article nor heard of his own company's scheme! He was not impressed with self build and Geoff and Sharon were not impressed with him. A change of building society quickly followed. They did, though, have to shop around to find a lender happy to meet the up front cost of their timber frame, and appropriate stage payments thereafter. Perversely, they discovered things might have been simpler had they not bought the plot outright, but borrowed for part of it, keeping some funds back to cover that initial timber frame expense.

FIGURE 21.2 The Jones' completed Medina Gimson timber frame home

Case Studies

The Jones moved into a mobile home on the site once the groundworks were finished and stayed there for ten months. Being right on site was desirable from the point of view of security, but also because they wanted to undertake a good deal of the work themselves. There were a number of minor hitches which seemed at the time like major problems but which were all successfully resolved. Geoff and Sharon have nothing but praise for their self build company, Medina Gimson, who patiently answered their many queries.

There was, however, one nasty scare just as the roof was completed. The building inspector announced it was too high. The prospect of re-building the roof was unthinkable, especially as it had been built according to the approved plans. The Jones handed this particularly hot potato over to Medina Gimson, who secured the council's agreement that the roof was, after all, acceptable.

The Jones moved into their house before everything inside was finished. For a while the main bedroom doubled as a living room. As painting and decorating progressed, so more of the house became lived in. By putting so much effort in themselves they have created a house they are both justifiably proud of, and

which is exactly what they wanted. Geoff and Sharon offer plenty of advice to other self builders. Sharon suggested putting extra cash aside at the start to cover bills that might need paying before a stage payment is reached. Keep track of your build costs and stick to your budget. Geoff emphasises the importance of choosing your timber frame company carefully so you know you have the backup of help and advice only a phone call away. A final word of advice for those prepared to get involved in the build themselves, 'be prepared for lots of hard work and little leisure time, but in the end, its worth it!'

KEY POINTS

◆ Do not just rely on papers and agents, get out and about in a car.

◆ Always check plot boundaries yourself.

◆ If the right plot appears to be sold, check anyway as sales do fall through.

◆ Check how long the planning permission has to run.

MIKE & SARAH COWLING, COLCHESTER

Mike had wanted to have his own house built for many years, ever since he had seen a Potton show house at the Ideal Home Show. He had always lived in the Colchester area, it was convenient for access to his work and, in the particular village where he most wanted to live, house prices always held up well, even during recessions, so he thought it would be a good investment. The main problem was that there seemed to be so little land around, plots hardly ever came on the market. At first Mike just registered with local estate agents but all he got sent was 'postage stamp' sized plots on sale for a lot of money. He also looked for plot adverts in local papers. For a period of four or five years there were a few possibilities around Colchester but nothing really suitable came up although, very usefully, during this time the Cowlings were able to save the money they would need to purchase a plot.

The Cowlings made sure all their family, friends and contacts knew they were looking for land. One of their friends was renting a cottage in the village where they wanted to live and noticed another cottage nearby being put on the market. That cottage had a wide side garden and more land to the rear. This sounded interesting and so Mike started to make enquiries. The cottage had been occupied by an elderly man who had just died and his family were selling the house. The piece of land on which the cottage stood amounted to two-and-a-half acres and was covered with old chicken sheds and dead trees. The side garden area, though, was about 100 feet wide, where it adjoined the lane, and opened out at the rear and so had potential to take another house next to the existing cottage with plenty of land for a good

sized garden. On checking the site with the council, Mike discovered that developers had been interested in the site and had, in fact, made a planning application a year earlier for permission to build on the land to the side of the cottage. That application had been refused, mainly because the access would have been sub-standard, emerging on to a winding narrow lane without adequate visibility. The access point serving the cottage,

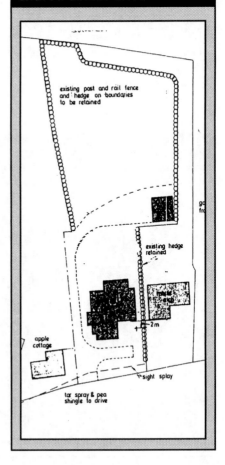

FIGURE 21.3 The Cowling's site layout plan showing the shared access drive

existing post and rail fence and hedge on boundaries to be retained

existing hedge retained

2m

apple cottage

sight splay

tar spray & pea shingle to drive

which was at the opposite end of the property to the side garden, was right on a blind bend and, consequently, very dangerous.

Since opportunities for building new houses were so few and far between, Mike and Sarah decided to pursue this site. They agreed with their friends to make a joint approach to the vendor; Mike and Sarah would try for a plot on the side garden land and, if successful, they would buy that and their friends would buy the adjoining cottage to live in. Clearly, the Cowlings did not want to go to the trouble and expense of pursuing a planning application only to see the plot and cottage sold to someone else. So, even though the housing market was not especially buoyant at the time, they offered the full asking price, but on the basis of a six month conditional contract. The purchase would only go ahead if Mike and Sarah could get

planning permission within six months. The vendors accepted and solicitors were instructed to draw up the necessary contract, which was signed a few months after the Cowlings had first seen the site.

Once the property was secured through the conditional contract, the Cowlings submitted an outline planning application to the council. However, this was quickly rejected by the council which turned down permission on grounds of highway safety. By this time they were already a few months into the contract period. Mike, Sarah and their friends re-considered and tried to come up with a solution to overcome the council's concern. They hit upon the idea of closing the existing highly dangerous access serving the cottage, re-locating the access point to the centre of the combined site and proposing a shared access to serve both the new house and the

FIGURE 21.4 Rear view of Mike and Sarah's completed Potton Gransden (Photo c/o Build It and Paul Dixon)

Case Studies

FIGURE 21.5 The side garden which turned into a perfect plot

existing cottage. Even this access would be sub-standard, but it would represent an improvement on the existing situation. Another outline planning application was submitted on that basis and this time it was approved by the council, just within time to beat the six month deadline.

The purchase was completed and at the same time the property title was split between the Cowlings and their friends on the basis of an agreed division of the site. Two separate titles were created; one for the cottage and one for the plot. Mike and Sarah were delighted not least because, by creating their own plot, they had achieved a saving of about one third on the price such a plot with planning permission would normally have sold for in that area.

The Cowlings went back to Potton to buy their timber frame house to build on the plot

and chose a modified version of the Gransden from Potton's Heritage range of house types. The house was built to look as if it had been standing for many years and features split level sitting room, large farmhouse-style kitchen, inglenook fireplace and vaulted ceiling in the master bedroom.

KEY POINTS

◆ Do not just rely on estate agents.

◆ Look for suitably wide gaps on the road frontage between houses.

◆ Houses on the market might have potential for plots within their grounds.

◆ Secure sites with conditional contracts or options before applying for permission.

PETER AND KARIN SKINNER

Peter and Karin Skinner had already renovated and built several houses when they decided to make one last move to the home that they and their young family would then stay in for good. Apart from working on their own homes, Peter's company, Cottage Construction, specialises in high quality barn conversions and renovations, and they wanted a similar house for themselves and so decided to look for both building plots and conversion opportunities. The Skinners had more or less made their minds up about where they wanted to live and, in anticipation of finding something in that area, had put their oldest son into a local village primary school. The position of the property was one of the prime criteria for their search as they did not want a town or estate location, preferring to have some space around them.

In early summer the Skinners started their search. They spoke to local estate agents giving them a wide brief from old houses for renovation, through conversions to building plots. During the summer Peter and Karin looked at a dozen or so properties, mainly older houses but including a few plots. Nothing really caught their imaginations. Peter was a regular reader of *Individual Homes* magazine and in the October issue land for sale section he noticed a barn for conversion very near the village where they wanted to live. Peter contacted the agent straight away, got the sales particulars and went down to see the barn. All that was left standing was a few walls of what had been a group of three single storey flint and brick barns around a central yard. Planning permission had been given some years earlier and demolition had taken place with the reusable materials stored on site. The Skinners met the agent to discuss the site and an offer. In order to buy the property and finance the rebuilding, they would have to sell their existing house, so they could not make an outright offer. There was not an asking price but offers were invited over a given figure. After the meeting, Peter and Karin did their sums and, knowing this was an ideal opportunity for them, quickly made a written offer at about the minimum figure specified by

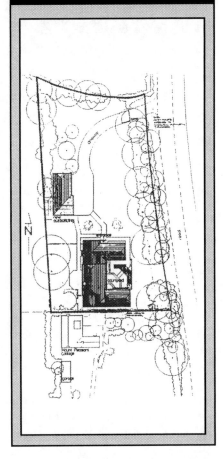

FIGURE 21.6 Site plan showing the layout of the re-built barns and new garage

FIGURE 21.7 The remains of the three barns as they were when bought by the Skinners

the vendor, based on a six month conditional contract. The contract offered included payment of a deposit, 50% of which would be non-returnable, with the balance payable when the Skinner's existing house was sold. This was accepted and solicitors were instructed to draw up the conditional contract.

Peter and Karin put their house on the market in November and within a matter of a month or so an offer at the asking price was made and accepted. All seemed well and it looked as though a six month period might not even be needed and the purchase of the barns could go through in the normal way. This was too good to be true and the Skinner's purchase was hit by two set backs. First, the buyers of their own house rang up one weekend to say they had now decided to buy a property elsewhere. Second, the council

questioned whether the planning permission on the barns had been implemented properly and so doubted whether it would remain valid when the five year period within which to start work ran out in the following February. The council also said it would not grant another permission and, without permission, the site would be worthless. Although they did not yet own the site, Peter co-operated with the vendor's agent in trying to resolve the planning situation. This involved first getting several approvals, including of building materials to be used and, being a builder, Peter was able to find and take samples for the council's approval. Quite rightly, the Skinners were not prepared to sign a contract committing themselves to the purchase until the council confirmed in writing that the permission was valid. Securing this

Case Studies

confirmation would mean more work would have to be carried out on the conversion and an agreement was reached with the vendor whereby Peter would dig the foundations. The permission was due to expire on 13th February and on 9th February Peter got the foundation trenches dug. Photographs were taken as a record of the work and the planning officer inspected the site a couple of days later. All concerned held their breath but on 15th February the council wrote confirming the permission was still valid.

Meanwhile, a second purchaser found for Peter and Karin's existing house fell by the wayside. The housing market was slow during the spring and, despite the Skinners's pushing their estate agents, there were no further offers.

The Skinners were on the verge of signing the contract when Peter noticed a discrepancy in the plans; the title plan did not seem to include a strip of land along the boundary next to the road. The solicitors could not immediately find out who owned the strip although it had been included within the boundaries of the site for many years. Peter and Karin's solicitor did not want them to sign until the ownership question was resolved. After further research it transpired that no one else was likely to be able to pop up and claim ownership of the strip. On that basis, the Skinners decided to go ahead and conditional contracts were finally exchanged in March.

Peter and Karin started feeling desperate as during the summer their house had not sold and the contract deadline was fast approaching. While they really needed the sale to take place to complete the purchase, this was their dream property and they were determined not to let it slip though their

FIGURE 21.8 Peter and Karin's conversion nearly complete

hands. Then towards the end of the summer the housing market picked up a little and they received three offers for their house. The Skinners accepted one of those offers with just six weeks to go to the deadline.

The sale was pushed through as quickly a possible and both purchase and sale were completed in the nick of time at the end of September.

Having bought the property, Peter and Karin with their four children, including newborn baby, moved into a mobile home on the site and Peter's company, Cottage Construction, has carried out the conversion to its usual high standard and specification. They have no regrets and believe all they went through was worth it to achieve the home they had dreamed of - a fitting tribute to their determination. (Cottage Construction can be contacted on 01273 401279).

KEY POINTS

◆ Find out as much as you can about the property to begin with.

◆ When you find what you want, do not hesitate - go for it.

◆ Be prepared to put up with some set backs and aggravation.

◆ Always keep the end in mind.

INDEX

Town and Country Planning
   Service (Northern
   Ireland), 52

town planners, 85

transport links, 45, 99

Tree Preservation Orders
   (TPOs), 87-90

trees, 66, 67, 87, 88

turning area, 23, 73

turn-key packages, 21

U.

Unitary Development Plan,
   53

unsaleable plots, 37, 38, 69

unusual designs, 21, 88

uplift clauses, 120

V.

valuation of plot, 97-107
   comparison with others,
   101
   residual method, 101,
   102, 103
   professional, 106
   rule-of-thumb method,
   101

valuers, 106. 111

VAT, 35

verges, 71

Village Envelope,
   same as Settlement
   Boundary,

W.

walls,
   external, 15
   maintenance, space for,
   23
   internal, 15

Water Service (Northern
   Ireland), 75

water supply, 77
   companies, 93

wayleaves, 93

wells and boreholes, 77

wet ground, 65, 66

wind, 65, 68

windows, 21, 92

Dear Reader

We hope you find this book as useful as have the many people who have contacted us since the first edition of How to **Find and Buy a Building Plot** was published in 1995. It has been fascinating to hear not only of the varied challenges people come across, but also of the creativity and determination they have used to overcome those challenges, resulting in many successful building projects. This has helped us revise the book to give you more plot-finding ideas and tips.

Some readers contacted us to ask where they could find more information on planning and, fortunately, we are able to recommend the companion volume to this book, **How to Get Planning Permission**. You will find information on its content and how to order a copy on page 3.

However, most readers who contact us do so because, having read our book, they want to find out if we will help them professionally, by giving them specific advice on their particular sites, problems or questions. Naturally, as practising planning consultants, we are generally able and pleased to do this. As a result, we have carried out Planning Appraisal Reports, to assess the likelihood of getting planning permission on particular sites, made and advised on planning applications and fought planning appeals where readers' planning applications have been refused by the council. Sometimes we are able to answer questions and deal with problems via our advice-by-post service. Not only have we been able to help readers all over the country but, again, the experiences have been fed back into this revision of the book.

So, if you do hit problems you cannot solve or want to get some professional advice on your project, you are welcome to get in contact with us. Also, if you have found or bought a plot in unusual circumstances, please write to us with your story. Contact numbers and an address are given on the next page.

We wish you success with your plot purchase and building project.

Roy Speer   *Michael Dade*

ROY SPEER AND MICHAEL DADE

Roy Speer and Michael Dade are consultants, writers and speakers on planning and land matters. Both are Chartered Surveyors with degrees in Estate Management. They run their own specialist town and country planning practice, carrying out a wide range of work throughout the country for individuals, builders/developers, landowners, businesses and other organisations.

Their consultancy work includes making and advising on planning applications, appeals and enforcement, giving evidence at hearings and public inquiries, carrying out Planning Appraisal Reports, and a useful advice-by-post service for readers. They have also developed the unique Planning Search for potential purchasers of plots and houses, to report on planned or likely development proposals in the immediate vicinity or area which might affect the value or enjoyment of the property, as this is not covered fully in solicitors' searches.

Roy Speer and **Michael Dade**
can be contacted on:
01273 843737 and 01825 890870
or
c/o **Stonepound Books,**
10 Stonepound Road,
Hassocks, West Sussex BN6 8PP